HIBERNIAN
The Easter Road Story

by
JOHN R. MACKAY

Foreword
DOUGLAS CROMB

JOHN DONALD PUBLISHERS LTD
EDINBURGH

ISBN 0 85976 426 5

British Libraty Cataloguing in Publication Data
A catlogue record for this book is available from the British Library.

Phototypeset by
WestKey Ltd, Falmouth, Cornwall
Printed & bound in Great Britain by
Bell & Bain Ltd, Glasgow

Foreword

It gives me great pleasure to write the foreword to a book that recalls so many great moments and occasions in our club's illustrious history.

Our new stadium at Easter Road heralds a bright new chapter in the history of our club, so it is a good time to take a look back and see what made us the way we are.

Memories are part of the game of football and we all have our favourites. Some will name the exploits of the Famous Five, others the genius of Baker, Stanton and Cormack, or perhaps the wayward skills of George Best. We all have memories that come from the emotional switchback of being a football supporter, be they the heights of beating Hearts 7–0 or the despair when not so long ago, we nearly lost our club.

My own treasure chest of memories comes from a lifetime of being a devoted Hibee, first from the terraces, now from the Chairman's seat in our wonderful new stadium. So it was with enthusiasm that I read John Mackay's book, for it enabled me to recapture many of the thrills of the past, reliving those that I have witnessed, and learning more about others from a more distant day that have been passed down by generations of Hibees.

This is a definitive, well researched work that makes an invaluable reference source for those who wish to learn more about our great club. I congratulate the author and commend it to our supporters.

DOUGLAS CROMB
Chairman Hibernian Football Club

Contents

Introduction

After *The Hibees* and *The Complete Story*, together with my involvement with the Hibs' programme during the late eighties, I did not envisaging doing another book about Hibs. Clearly I will never now get a job as a prophet, and that is for a number of reasons:

Firstly, the decision of the board in 1994 to remain at Easter Road and redevelop the stadium has been welcomed by the vast majority of Hibs' supporters. The Hibernian F.C. Museum project is a part of that and I am delighted to have been invited to join that team. The present board are a pleasure to work with, and the atmosphere at Easter Road is more constructive and fan-friendly than I have experienced. The stadium refurbishment provides an ideal break point to look back on what has happened to Hibs at Easter Road in its previous guises (and elsewhere).

Secondly, a lot has happened since *The Hibees*, in particular the episode which involved a take-over in 1987, two share issues in 1988 and 1989, an attempted liquidation in 1990 and receivership in 1991 before an eleventh hour rescue. *The Complete Story* had to be finished during the Mercer episode, and therefore had to be politic in its attitude to that unfortunate affair, and enough time has now probably passed for the story to be documented more dispassionately than in 1990.

Thirdly, there is a new generation of Hibs fans who probably do not have a Hibs' book which includes the recent past with which they can identify. The chapters on the last ten years or so, since the publication of *The Hibees*, are therefore fuller covered than the older history, which is in turn structured differently than before. Thirty-five per cent of this book effectively covers new ground therefore, and most of the illustrations are new, in many cases courtesy of the Hibs

Museum. In addition, the majority of the various statistics in both previous books are updated for the years since 1985.

Acknowledgements

Douglas Cromb, Allan Munro, the Hibernian Museum Committee, Bill Brady (Scotsman Publications Photo Sales), Fraser Thom, Graeme Mackay, David Ferguson.

Full team photograph for season 1995-96

— 1 —
EARLY DAYS

When football arrived in Scotland from the south in the 1860s, it came with a ready-made class system; from the start, the private schools, notably in Edinburgh, adopted the form played by the pupils at Rugby, whereas the industrial areas of Clydeside played the version of England's industrial north, the association code. In Edinburgh, the first association match did not take place until the last few days of 1873, and even then it was two teams from Glasgow, both from Queens Park, who demonstrated the art of kicking the ball at Royal High School's rugby ground.

The visit of Queens Park aroused some interest among the local youngsters, and in 1874 there were a few clubs. Rules were vague—clubs tended to have their own—and with clouded memories of the Queens Park demo, and the influence of the rugby clubs around, a sort of hybrid game based on association rules but involving outfield players handling the ball too, grew up. Some years later, when clubs like Hibs and Hearts were in the habit of playing teams from Glasgow, commentators still remarked the preference of Edinburgh players to pick the ball up.

Unable to obtain fixtures against Edinburgh's rugby elite, the few association clubs found life difficult, and few survived—the most notable being the 3rd Edinburgh Rifle Volunteers. The most notable failure, at least in hindsight, was a club called White Star; they seem to have folded in mid-1875, and, as mentioned in John Rafferty's '100 Years of Scottish Football', the break-up spawned both Hibs and Hearts in August 1875. A number of other clubs came into existence in a surge of popularity that year, and the Edinburgh F.A. was formed, and so the scarcity of fixtures which had blighted earlier attempts was avoided.

Hibs were formed by members of the Catholic Young Men's Society attached to St. Patrick's Church in the Cowgate, and only practising members of the congregation could join. The name Hibernian was chosen, history says by Michael Whelehan, who was elected the first captain, to reflect their Irish descent. As with most of the other clubs, they played at the Meadows—their tract seems to have run along where the present tennis courts are, and they chose green and white as their colours from the start—white guernseys with *Erin-go Bragh*, which means 'Ireland for Ever' on the left breast, and green and white striped knickerbockers.

These colours do not seem to have clashed with anybody else's. For one thing, nobody else would play them. The Edinburgh F.A. turned them down on the grounds they would have to join the Scottish F.A. first, and the Scottish F.A. did likewise on the grounds they were not Scottish but Irish. Clubs were warned not to play them, and so Saturdays up till Christmas were taken up with endless practices—as were Tuesday and Thursday evenings—on the unlit Meadows. Christmas Day saw their first match recorded by *The Scotsman*, resulting in a 1–0 defeat by the Heart of Midlothian. After that, there were occasional games until the end of the season, by when, with the help of a petition signed by most local players, Hibs had been admitted to the hallowed ranks of the Edinburgh F.A.

The pitches on the Meadows were of various sizes, from a hundred to nearly two hundred yards long, and from thirty or forty yards wide to twice that amount. Goalposts were connected at the top by a tape rather than a bar, so that it was by no means rare for the ball to go over the tape only because of a judicious push of a post at the vital moment. Crowd encroachment was commonplace, referees came one from each club, so that neither was ever accused of impartiality, and in any case the rules far from uniform, never mind clear. The games were taken seriously, reports of bad language, violence, etc. the norm, and in particular, games involving the local Irish community, not the most popular group in the city, were played out with some intensity.

Hibs second season was a little frustrating for their supporters, but less so than for the adherents of the Heart of Midlothian, and with only one year behind them, did feature one or two firsts. Although they were getting there, Hibs had not broken through the SFA bureaucracy quickly enough to be allowed to play in the Scottish Cup, but they did reach the semi-final of the Edinburgh Cup, where they lost

1–0 to Hanover. Heart of Midlothian however broke up, had to scratch from the national competition, and were not included in the local one. In October, Hibs played St. Andrews, another Edinburgh team, who now included Tom Purdie, the ex-captain of Heart of Midlothian, and who were later to be persuaded by him to change their name to Heart of Midlothian. This had been done by the time Hibs beat them, for the first time, in February 1877.

As the number of clubs increased, the 3rd ERV led the exodus from the Meadows by moving to their training ground at what was Powburn Village (and is now the shops at Mayfield Road in Newington.) For Hibs, the main excitement was their first Scottish Cup venture, and they did well enough to go further than any Edinburgh side so far—Hearts were beaten in Hibs' first tie, then Hanover and Swifts in further regional rounds before Hibs had to undertake their first trip outside the city, to Thornliebank. *The Scotsman* reported the game twice, as 2–1 and 2–0 wins for Hibs, but the SFA decided that as it had been drawn, a replay should take place. Because of the importance of this event, it took place at 3rd ERV's premises at Powburn, and another draw resulted, so both clubs went through. This odd rule sometimes meant that three clubs reached the semi-finals, but it was not to concern Hibs in 1877–78, because next time out, and back in Glasgow, they lost 3–0 to South-Western of Govan. In addition, three Hibs' men, Byrne, Rourke and Quinn, were included in the Edinburgh F.A. teams which did well against Glasgow giants Queens Park and 3rd Lanark.

By now, association football was claiming much of the attention previously given only to rugby, and Hibs and Hearts were emerging from the welter of local sides which had come on stream in the previous two or three years, but few could have foreseen the extraordinary saga the two clubs played out in the spring of 1878 in the Edinburgh Cup final.

The first match took place on February 9th, before 'a good number' of spectators at Mayfield, as Powburn was now known, and ended goalless, with Hibs having two scores disallowed. A week later, a 1–1 draw resulted at the same venue with a 1000 crowd; unfortunately, the possibility of extra time was left to the two captains, and with Hibs finishing the stronger, Hearts' captain Purdie refused, incurring considerable wrath amongst the Hibs' supporters. To avoid further trouble, admission prices were raised for the third game, again at Mayfield, and a crowd of 1200 saw the kick-off, a figure that was nearly doubled by an invasion from without during the second half. The score was 1–1 again.

So a fourth game was needed, and it took place at Merchiston, and ended 1–1 yet again, despite an extra half hour. The fifth game at last broke the deadlock, on April 18th, back at Mayfield and more than two months after the first game. For some reason, Hibs seem to have been clear favourites, but Hearts won 3–2. It seems that not all the spectators were happy about this, and the Hearts' captain had to take refuge in a house after being set upon on his way back to the city.

Powderhall

Hibs have had essentially only five grounds during their long history, but they played at four of them in successive seasons. The pressure on the Meadows was becoming ever greater, both from too many clubs trying to find space, with the attendant disputes, and the fact that the actual ground had suffered from too many games. A number of clubs moved away from the central venue, and Hibs moved into Powderhall Grounds in Bonnington Road for 1878–79. Their club house was still in St Mary's Street, a factor of no insignificance given the transport difficulties, and the habit of travelling back from games, soaking or otherwise, with football clothes under normal day wear. Related illnesses were common and even some fatalities occurred.

Hibs' stay at Powderhall was notable for two games in particular— an early attempt to play under artificial light, and a bizarre Scottish Cup-tie against Helensburgh. In addition, however, they showed themselves the capital's top dogs by winning the Edinburgh Cup, beating Hearts 2–0 in a replay at Corstorphine, and defeating the 3rd ERV, still then regarded as the top club despite having left the association over a dispute, In a curious match where Hibs led 3–0, at which point two of their opponents had to retire ill, and a mixed friendly was arranged for the remainder of the ninety minutes.

It was at the end of October that a few hundred spectators came along to see 'Hibernians v. an Association team (by electric light)', following a similar experiment at Third Lanark's Cathkin a few days earlier. Three Siemens dynamo electric machines provided a total of about 8400 watts. One of the smaller ones failed to function from the outset, but the other two provided light for about an hour, when a strap broke, and the game was concluded virtually in darkness. Hibs won 3–0, and apparently no further similar attempts were made.

The cup-tie against Helensburgh demonstrated the bickering which was all too common in the pre-Farry days when the rule book was less than definitive. The tie was scheduled for the Saturday before Christmas, the crowd was assembled, and Hibs were on the admittedly treacherous pitch when their visitors, stripped for action, decided against taking part, and offered to play a friendly instead. Hibs were having none of that, and a practice was hastily arranged for their players.

The tie took place several weeks later. Helensburgh were denied a goal because 'something disallowable had taken place', but nevertheless were ahead at half-time. Shortly afterwards, the visiting goalkeeper came out to intercept the ball, failed miserably to do so, and was unable to regain his ground before an unscrupulous Hibs player put the ball between the posts. An argument ensued as to whether this was fair, and Hibs had to accept the rather unsatisfactory compromise of a corner, and felt even more aggrieved when Helensburgh scored the winning goal a little later.

Mayfield

The entertainment at Powderhall had not finished for Hibs' supporters as we will see, but the summer of 1879 saw them move out to Mayfield, occupying what is now the eastern parts of West Savile Terrace and McDowell Road. The clubhouse was still at St Mary's Street, but at least there was a stripping box at Newington. The inaugurating of this facility was to be performed by Glasgow Rangers—at that time they were usually called that to distinguish them from the Edinburgh club of the same name rather than from ignorance—and the visit was much anticipated. However, the great day was a flop, as Rangers were unable to raise a team. The honour went instead therefore to the opponents of a week later, Kilmarnock Athletic, who returned the hospitality by beating Hibs by six goals to one.

The Powderhall reference was to that season's Scottish Cup match away to Hearts, who had moved into Hibs' previous home.

The appeal of Hibs is worldwide

Unfortunately, came the appointed hour, it seems that Hearts had not paid the rent, and their landlords with the help of the police took possession of the pay-boxes and ejected them. The game was re-scheduled for Mayfield, where there was another touch of farce, this time an argument about kick-off time. Hearts turned up at one o'clock, kicked off and claimed the tie, and Hibs did likewise at three, before actually playing the recently formed St Bernards instead.

The tie was played at last at Mayfield at the third attempt, albeit late, because the referee turned up twenty minutes after kick-off time. By the time Hearts scored their only goal, to make it 2–1, it was pitch dark, then with the ball in the possession of the Hearts goalkeeper Reid, several hundred spectators came on to the pitch to assist their heroes, no goal was the verdict and Hibs went through. They were to go even further this time than last, with wins over Park Grove, an imaginatively named team from Govan, on the two draw rule, and Mauchline, an even more imaginatively named team from Mauchline, before they lost in the sixth round at Dumbarton.

— 2 —

THE FIRST EASTER ROAD

Hibs were to stay at Mayfield for less than a season, because the new ground they had been preparing at Easter Road was ready by March; Thornliebank, an attractive side who beat Hibs 3–0, were the last visitors at Mayfield, Hanover, a local XI were the first visitors at Easter Road and lost 5–0.

The new ground at Easter Road was not on the site of the present stadium, but a few hundred yards south, across the railway line. The halfway line would roughly be the line of Bothwell Street from the bend in the road to the railway footbridge; the far corner of the ground reached W & A K Johnstone's Edina map-printing works and the main entrance was the lane beside the church nowadays the entrance to the Hibs' Supporters' Club in Sunnyside.

The summer of 1880 saw some other changes to Hibs. Michael Whelehan moved over for Paddy Cavanagh to become captain and the

1884–85 Membership card. (courtesy HFC Museum)

green and white hoops which had been Hibs' colours since 1876 gave way to plain green jerseys. They nearly failed to see the light of day, however, courtesy of their city rivals.

Hibs had beaten Dunfermline 6–3 in the spring and so had now won the Edinburgh Cup twice, and were favourites for the hat-trick, which would enable them to keep the trophy. Hearts were determined to stop them, firstly by putting down a motion that Hibs be expelled from the Edinburgh F.A. because of the rough behaviour of their players on the pitch and their supporters off it. This sort of thing was of course alien to Hearts and their adherents. The vote was ten for, ten against and five abstentions, and so Hibs remained in the fold by the narrowest of squeaks.

Hearts did manage to beat Hibs in a regional round of the Scottish Cup, but this year it was the local one that mattered, and the national tie set up a showdown that attracted a crowd of 7,000 at Powderhall—and that was before even more broke in. Hearts scored first, Cox equalised for Hibs, and Lee scored twice in a minute near the end to restore the natural order of things. Hearts still were not finished with the Edinburgh Cup however—they protested in vain that Hibs had fielded a player who was not local—it is not clear if that broke any actual rule—and for good measure or spite their president wrote to *The Scotsman* to say that the score was only 2–1 anyway.

Thus over several hurdles, Hibs only found one more difficult one in winning the trophy again—St Bernards in the final, since the Saints led 4–0 with an hour gone. Fortunately, Hibs scrambled back to 4–4, and scored the only goal in the replay, so the silverware was theirs; the Edinburgh Cup, together with the equivalent trophy for Second XIs, have been looked after ever since in St Patrick's Church.

By the new season, 1881–82, Hibs were attracting substantial crowds, as they became popular with the inhabitants of Leith, as well as their traditional Irish support, and were establishing the link by which they are nowadays regarded as a Leith team. Dean of Guild approval was obtained for Hibs' first grandstand in September, and the it was opened three weeks later, for the Hibs v St Bernards cup-tie and a 5,000 crowd. Hibs went on to lose to old rivals Dumbarton 6–2 in the sixth round, after escaping ignominy with a 4–4 draw at West Benhar a round earlier, but won the East of Scotland Shield, the replacement for the Edinburgh Cup, with another win against St Bernards.

Sunday School Picnic

Like all successful teams, the time came for rebuilding the team, and Hibs had a mediocre season in 1882–83; the position was not helped by their first loss of two players, Cox and McKernan, moving to England. Hibs even relinquished their grip on the East of Scotland Shield, when the difficulty of putting out a credible team persuaded them to have the final postponed. When this was refused, Hibs scratched, leaving Edinburgh University, who had beaten Hearts 5–2 in the other semi-final, with the trophy for the only time.

Many of their team problems were however solved at one fortuitous stroke. Hibs were still the team of St Patrick's first and foremost, and as part of a Sunday School trip to Ayrshire in the spring of 1883, a scratch church—or Hibs—team took on a local team at Lugar, as a result of which the entire Lugar half-back line of McGhee, McGinn and McLaren came to Easter Road. James McLaren was the 'Auld General', crafty rather than fast, who would surely have been the first Hibs' man to be capped had there been any way of finding out whether he was Scottish or Irish. Jim McGhee became the Easter Road captain, strong in midfield and immensely popular—much like Pat Stanton of later vintage, and praise comes no higher. Between them, they formed the backbone of the Hibs team which became increasingly successful, and made Easter Road a place where few opponents looked 'to get a result' as they didn't say in these times. But it was not obvious after their debut, a 10–2 defeat from Queen's Park.

They were also to be the backbone of the Edinburgh F.A. side, but not until the small minds who opposed Hibs within that body had another fling. With Hibs now far and away the best side in the area, the EFA was persuaded to ban imported players from Shield matches, despite McGhee and McLaren having already played for the Edinburgh F.A. side, and it took a clever piece of parliamentary subterfuge to get a vote passed rescinding the ban. The effect was much as their opponents feared—Hibs beat St. Bernards 7–0 in the Shield final.

They also managed a further step in the Scottish Cup—results included an early win, by 4–1, against Hearts, and a notable 6–1 win over Battlefield 'who had a good game, but had hard luck in scoring' in the quarter-finals. This brought the mighty Queens Park, a much bigger and heavier team even than Hibs, to Easter Road for Hibs' first semi-final, but, especially as Hibs had lost 5–1 to the men from Hampden a few weeks earlier, it was little surprise that 'at no period can the contest be said to have been keen' and another 5–1 defeat resulted.

Heartache

A year later, and some more progress, as Hibs reached the semi-finals again, pretty uneventfully, and this time recorded only a narrow defeat, 3–2, to a late winner. This seemed partly because they had continued to improve, and partly because their opponents this time were Renton, not Queens Park.

There was not even the customary defeat of Hearts to savour. The vexed subject of professionalism, its effect on smaller clubs, the drift of players south and the moral position, was virtually the only topic of conversation in football circles, while all the clubs who voted for the amateur *status quo* carried on paying their players under the counter as before. But Hearts were accused of professionalism, to wit, paying their players for a cup-tie against Dunfermline, and were expelled from the Scottish Cup and the SFA. Dunfermline obviously felt a grievance, perhaps because of the 11–1 scoreline; for their part, Hearts clearly learned a lesson, as they have never faced a similar charge since.

They were admitted back into the fold a couple of months later, and somehow had managed to retain their place in the Shield, so that Hibs had to beat them in this competition en route to winning it again, this time by 3–2 against the University.

By now, Hibs had achieved a new status; a second stand had been built opposite the first, and some wooden terracing provided a better view for the large crowds, typically four or five thousand, which now attended Easter Road for the bigger games. Gone was the novelty of the west's bigger clubs coming to the ground—now there was the expectation of beating them. Hibs had two core supports—their new friends in Leith, and the Catholic population of Scotland; they played far and wide in support of Catholic charities, and recruited as widely.

Also, far from being local outcasts, the Edinburgh F.A. was now proud of them. Hibs, according to the chairman at the annual prize giving, 'now occupied the position of premier club in Scotland, Cambridge University alone beating them in the United Kingdom'. This was perhaps stretching the point, as Hibs had yet to beat Queens Park for example, but even that was redressed early in 1985–86, when the Easter Road side scored a deserved if surprising 2–1 victory.

Other notable scalps included Renton, Dumbarton and Cambuslang. Dumbarton came to Easter Road in the fifth round of the Scottish Cup, and with the pitch a perfect quagmire, the Boghead side were in their element. They also led 3–1 at one point, a lead which they fell back on as was their habit—an unusual one in 1886—and Hibs came back to win 4–3 amid scenes of the wildest excitement, skipper McGhee being mobbed when he scored the winner.

It was one of these occasions when the odd rules of the competition resulted in five teams being left in whatever a round with five teams is called. Hibs played Cambuslang in the only tie, winning 3–2, to set up another semi-final opportunity. Again Hibs had home advantage, again Renton provided the opposition, again expectations were high, and again they were dashed as the visitors held on to an early two goal lead to go through. It was scant consolation to win both local finals against Hearts.

Willie Groves

Help was at hand, though, in the person of Willie Groves, a teenager who had come into the Hibs' team in the spring of 1886. Groves was of English extraction, his grandfather having been seconded from the Metropolitan Police to help the Edinburgh force catch Deacon Brodie. He also stood out immediately in the big physical Hibs team, a player of athletic grace, genuine pace, wonderful dribbling and a bewildering swerve. He has been acclaimed along with Bobby Walker of Hearts as the outstanding player of nineteenth century Edinburgh football. Although he left Hibs while still in his teens, like Joe Baker later 'Darlin' Willie' never lost the affection of the Easter Road fans.

With goals coming freely, Hibs cruised through the early rounds of the Scottish Cup as well as beating Bolton Wanderers, Stoke and

Middlesbro'(by 10–2). To reach the sixth round, they recorded wins against Durhamtown Rangers, Mossend Swifts, Hearts and Queen of the South Wanderers, of whom only Mossend offered a challenge. The West Calder side were in the middle of an eight year run with only one home defeat, and if most of the top sides chose not to visit them, then some like Everton had. It seems likely that the dreadful ground conditions and the intimidation of the local partisans on opponents and referees alike had as much to do with both their fixture card and their success rate as their robust tactics on the field, and even Hibs, a top team and well equipped to take care of themselves, were relieved to come away with a 1–1 draw. Even the replay was no picnic, the roughness of the Swifts' play causing no end of bother before Hibs got through on a 3–0 scoreline.Later in the season, Hibs had another roughhouse to contend with in the same locality, beating West Calder 3–1 in a shield tie.

Hibs' sixth round—or quarter final—tie was one of only a handful of Scottish Cup matches ever to have taken place on Christmas Day. The rain and sleet that had fallen all week had frozen to form pools of ice, and the wonder was that the captains agreed to play. Hibs skated

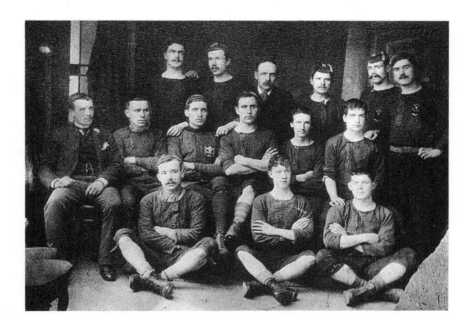

The Hibs team of 1887

to a 2–1 interval lead, and survived a lot of pressure thereafter to reach their fourth consecutive semi-final.

Surely this time Hibs would make it. With their record, there was at least no grounds for complacency, and Hibs took the field, once again at Easter Road, against Vale of Leven in determined mood. They shrugged off McNicol's opening goal, and Groves equalised just before the interval. In the second half, the ball was forced through the Vale goal during a scrimmage, and scarcely had the cheering died down when Montgomery made it 3–1, to ensure that at last Hibs reached the final.

Or at least they thought they had. There was good and bad news during the following week. The good was that Dumbarton surprisingly beat Queens Park in the other semi-final—surely they would be less formidable opponents; the bad was that Vale of Leven had protested that Willie Groves had received payment for Hibs, and so the semi-final result should not stand. Displaying the organisational skills which were the hallmark of the times, the SFA arranged the hearing for two days after the final.

Meanwhile, it was a day out at Hampden on February 12th; a crowd of 12,000 attended, aided to the ground by a fleet of cabs and a train of freight wagons with two engines plying the new Cathcart circle railway line to Crosshills near Hampden. The pitch was icy, and Dumbarton seemed to adapt better to it; they had the better of the first half and Aitken gave them a lead early in the second. Again, Dumbarton fell back in defence, but for a while Hibs seemed unable to do anything about it, despite strenuous efforts. Then suddenly, the Dumbarton goalkeeper completely misjudged a fairly ordinary shot from Clark, and the scores were level. Thus encouraged, Hibs redoubled their efforts, and Groves left defenders in his wake as he swerved through the defence and squared for Lafferty, yet another recruit from Lugar, to score what proved to be the winner. Hibs knew that they had been a little lucky to win on the day, but that failed to dampen the celebrations first in Glasgow, and later when they brought the trophy back to St Mary's Street Hall.

There was still the matter of Vale of Leven's protest, of course. The facts that Vale were unable to offer any evidence and that Hibs were notwithstanding only cleared on the casting vote of the chairman spoke volumes about the attitudes and prejudices of those involved.

On a happier note, there were further local final wins against Hearts, 3–0 in the Shield and an entertaining 7–1 in the Charity Cup.

World to Conquer

As Scottish Cup winners, Hibs seemed to have reached the pinnacle of achievement, but their ambitions stretched even further. In August 1887 they challenged Preston North End's 'Old Invincibles' for the Association Football Championship of the World. Six goal reverses from Queen of the South Wanderers and Renton were not the ideal preparation, but came the day came the team, and a huge crowd witnessed the first Easter Road's most historic afternoon.

The game was fast and furiously contested. McGhee put Hibs ahead in the first half with a long shot, and McLaren hit another three minutes after half-time, taking the ball on the drop. From then it was all Preston and mostly Goodall. Dewhurst did hit the bar, but Goodall struck both the post and the bar before heading Preston's first goal past Tobin, and had a further effort scrambled off the Hibs' line, before the whistle finally ended Hibs' anxiety and started their celebrations.

As a measure of Hibs' achievement, just one week later Preston were beating Rangers 8–1 at Ibrox when a crowd invasion ensured an early conclusion. On the other hand, it was perhaps as well that Hibs' opponents were Preston, who were not F.A.Cupholders, since Aston Villa, who were, had beaten Hibs 8–3 at Easter Road on New Year's Day.

Despite their historic win, the signs were that Hibs, with some new faces in Gallagher, Cox and McKeown, were not quite the team they had been. They lost to Hearts in the third round of the Scottish Cup, and in a real upset, lost to Mossend in the Shield final. But any problems which they thought they had were as nothing when real trouble came along; Hibs had no inkling of what was to come when they played Cowlairs at Janefield for the benefit of a new Catholic club called Celtic.

Celtic

One of those who had watched Hibs in several of their charity games in the west was a Marist brother called Walfrid, who recognised the income generating potential of a team created for that specific purpose, and to that end, and via a handbill which promoted the twin aims of providing for Glasgow's Catholic poor and doing for young Catholics in the west 'what Hibernians have been doing in the east', established Celtic.

Celtic's first game in May 1888 was—coincidentally considering future rivalries—against Rangers; their opening game the following season was against Hibs at Janefield. Working as far as possible from the adage that one good turn deserves another, Celtic fielded no fewer than six of Hibs' first team regulars, including Groves and McLaren, and won 3–2. More moves were to follow, and Celtic were to field as many as ten ex-Hibs men on occasion. Coleman and Dunbar were generally held responsible for the mass migration, although many people were at a loss to understand why there were so many willing defectors from the country's top club to a brand new outfit still with everything to prove, within the amateur constraints of the game.

Hibs' supporters back in Edinburgh had few doubts when Celtic came to Easter Road in October, as many a subtle comment from the touch line indicated. Celtic's three first half goals came from Dunbar (2) and Coleman, and were received in total silence, whereas the noise when Groves was charged over when apparently in the act of scoring raised the roof. Three times in the second half the pitch was invaded, and every Celtic player surrounded by an unfriendly mob, until, on a pre-arranged signal with ten minutes left, the Celtic party caught the crowd on the hop by sprinting from the pitch for their train It was to be several years before Celtic turned out at Easter Road again, and even then unwillingly.

The rest of the season was desperate; most games were against comparatively minor opposition, Dundee Harp, Glasgow Thistle, Leith Harp etc., and in their remaining games against the bigger teams Hibs recorded big losses, such as 7–1 against Queens Park and 7–2 against Third Lanark. When they played Leith Athletic, they had to recruit players from the crowd, and soon the crowds were scarcely big enough to do that. To make matters worse, Cox and McMahon went to Burnley. Hibs fall had been even more spectacular than their rise.

They even had the support of their main rivals; at the Heart of Midlothian Annual Concert (in the Oddfellows Hall) the chairman noted that 'for various circumstances which all deplored and were familiar with, Hibernians have been weakened this season and from the quarter least expected. Better things might have been looked for from the club from which Hibernians received their blow, and if it was a ray of consolation, it was the universal sympathy expressed for them'- a passage as yet unmentioned in histories of Celtic!

It might have been thought that things could hardly get worse, but they did. Within a year, the Celtic committee had squabbled and split. The minority group tried to coax Hibs through to Glasgow, and when that failed, they formed another new club. Glasgow Hibernians took the field for their opening engagements with another four Hibs' men in their ranks—Tobin, the goalkeeper of the cupwinning team, Clark, Smith and Coyle.

Despite that, Hibs still had some good players, notably McGhee, Sandy McMahon who returned from a sojourn with Burnley a much improved player—he later played for Scotland—and Naughton, who had returned from Celtic. They had a reasonable sequence of results too, although not including any of the country's biggest guns, and they reached the quarter finals of the Scottish Cup. Their progress to that stage was by defeating Armadale, Mossend, Dunfermline Athletic and Queen of the South Wanderers, as well as a bye, and if the two wins in West Lothian were hard fought, and the win against Dunfermline only achieved after a draw, then the replay against the Fifers brought a win by 11–1, and the tie against the Dumfriesians a 7–3 one. When Hibs did meet a team with some class, Abercorn, their effort was not enough, and they were comprehensively beaten by six goals to two.

Unfortunately that was their swansong. By the following autumn, they were in fear of losing their ground to developers as the city expanded, and tried to bribe the owners to transfer the lease of Logie Green to them—to no avail. Their fears were well grounded, and a few weeks later, they were homeless. The last game at Easter Road was a Scottish Cup match against Dumbarton, in which Hibs lost a goal in the first minute and nine in all.

Things went downhill rapidly. Hibs played a number of games on opponents' grounds, the last of which was on Valentine's Day 1891, when Leith Athletic played them at Bank Park for Hibs' benefit, and won 6–1. Neither McGhee nor McMahon turned up. One group did try to carry on, under the name Leith Hibernians, at Hawkhill, but they managed only one game there. They managed only two wins in just over a dozen games, against a scratch team of St Bernards players who had escaped the suspension which had hit the Logie Green club, and Motherwell. Their last throes were at the Leith Athletic fives on July 18th.

Furthermore, following the Renton scandal, when they were banned for doctoring their accounts to cover up their paying their players, all clubs had to submit accounts to the S.F.A. for scrutiny. Cowlairs were suspended as a result, and Hibs and Glasgow hibs would have been had these clubs not been considered already defunct. In August, Hibs were removed from the roll of members of the S.F.A. and the Edinburgh F.A. It looked like the end of the road.

— 3 —

THE SECOND EASTER ROAD

The year 1891 was hardly the golden age of Edinburgh football. Apart from Hibs having been forced out of business, St Bernards had been suspended for about a year for rather naively playing the banned Renton under the name of Edinburgh Saints, and thereby allowed Hearts to become undisputed top dogs in the city. However, even as Leith Hibernians were struggling on, there were moves behind the scenes to revive Hibs. A meeting on 7th March 1892 of those 'favourable to the resuscitation of the Club' was held, and the first £25 of a guarantee fund was raised. Likely helpers were circularised in an attempt to get the club back in business for the start of 1892–93 season, and the fund was brought up to £100, but it seemed to stick there. In October, a public meeting was called in St Mary's Street Hall to enlist wider support 'to resuscitate the old Hibernians football club'.

It was at that meeting that the club was re-formed, this time along non-sectarian lines, although a motion that Irishmen would get precedence was passed a few months later. No contact had been made, or was intended, with the old committee. The first meeting of the new club took place on December 12th, when Nicholas Burke was elected president, with the other office-bearers Thomas Flood, Charlie Sandilands, C F Perry and Philip Farmer, Great-Grand Uncle of the club's present owner, as treasurer. A local councillor, Mr Hunter, negotiated a ground a few hundred yards north of where the old Hibs had had their ground in Easter Road.

The pitch was not exactly ideal. Access was along a single narrow lane from Easter Road, and the ground might have been called Drum Park, in which it was situated. Instead, it was named Hibernian Park, and became known as Easter Road partly because Albion Road had not been built by that time and partly because there was already some

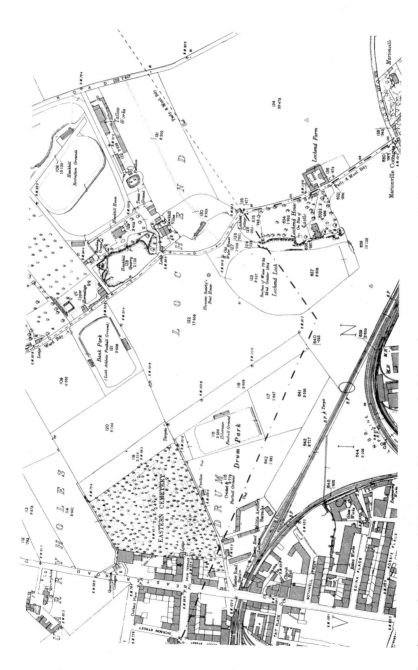

Map showing the newly established second Easter Road, close to Leith Athletic's Bank Park and Hawkhill

attachment to the name Easter Road. Moreover, it was on a considerable slope, about twice the gradient of the 1924–1995 pitch, and was only a couple of hundred yards from Leith Athletic's Bank Park. That ground was situated on the opposite side of what is now Hawkhill Avenue, at the point where it was later to be bisected by the railway line. Leith had been filling the vacuum on the north and east of the city with some success, and it was by no means clear at the outset how long it would take Hibs to re-attract all of their erstwhile support. As always, finance was all-important, and so the new pitch was leased to a farmer for grazing cattle when not in use.

Work started immediately to get the pitch and facilities up to scratch. A paling was built round the playing area, and a grandstand, which became known fondly as the Eggbox, on the eastern side of the ground. This stretched only along the lower half of the pitch, finishing just above the halfway line, and, facing westwards, exposed those within occasionally to the problems of seeing into a setting sun, and more frequently to the rain and gales that whipped in regularly from Greenland—much as at the present time on the east terrace. But football fans were a hardy breed in 1892 and there was not a golden cagoule in sight.

A stripping box stood further up the same side of the pitch, separate from the grandstand à la the famous Broomfield cricket pavilion, and where the modern facilities had been extended to combs and looking glasses by the time the first 'new' Hibs team met to play Clyde on February 4th 1893. What they thought about of the cows having been there first was not recorded. Hibs had assembled a fair team for the occasion, including Peter Meechan and Paddy Murray who were later to play for Scotland, and they held their opponents to a 4–3 scoreline. Hibs achieved wins against Dumbarton, St Mirren and Leith Athletic, which they thought highly satisfactory.

A lot had happened while Hibs were immersed in their own troubles; the Scottish League had been formed, and included the sides mentioned in the last paragraph. The Scottish Cup had also been revamped, with a qualifying competition, so that in 1893–94 Hibs had to play in the qualifying competition for the only time and went out in the third round to Vale of Leven. The penalty kick had been introduced as a deterrent to deliberate handball on the line, and professionalism finally adopted in 1893, nine years after it had been accepted in England. It was small wonder that in the same year Queens Park were the last amateur team to win the Scottish Cup.

In their two months of active play, however, Hibs had shown that they were already equipped to play at league level, and they were one of the founder members of the Second Division of the league, which was formed in 1893 mainly by Airdrieonians.

The Second Division

They won the inaugural competition too, by two points from Cowlairs, and with nine wins and five defeats in games against First Division teams, were clearly the best equipped for promotion. Unfortunately, promotion was not automatic, but in the hands of the First Division sides, and there was outrage at Easter Road when Clyde moved up in preference to Hibs, or for that matter Cowlairs. It was widely believed that the threat that Hibs seemed to pose to two of their prospective opponents in particular, on geographical and ethnic grounds respectively, had caused much lobbying against them.

Hibs' superiority in their second season in the Second Division was even more pronounced, with a margin of eight points after the eighteen game programme. This time their claim for promotion was irresistible, and they joined the elite of Division One. But the depth of feeling against Celtic was not forgotten, and the Glasgow side had to visit Easter Road in the cup, something they had declined to do socially for more than six years. A huge crowd of fifteen thousand in specially built stands thought they had seen Celtic get what they deserved, and they were dismayed when an appeal about a Hibs player having played in a junior game the previous year was upheld. The result was in a replay. Surely Celtic have never been as unpopular as when they returned to Easter Road to be booed and jeered throughout a 2–0 win.

Hibs made an immediate impact in 1895–96, their first season in the first division. They started with seven goals against Third Lanark at Cathkin, took eleven points out of a possible first twelve, before dropping the odd game to finish as runners up to Hearts. Top scorer Martin had gone to Celtic, but his promising young replacement Kennedy scored hat-tricks against Dumbarton and Hearts. Moreover, Paddy Murray and Bobby Neil were capped by Scotland, which underlined Hibs' return to top-flight status.

The Logie Green final

Hibs also had an impressive cup run, in which they defeated East Stirlingshire and Raith Rovers before their first cup visit to Ibrox. This was a fierce battle, in which Rangers missed two penalties before Hibs won through by the odd goal in five. The home keeper, Bell, took it all very badly—he was reported to have dressed in silence, left the ground alone and never to have been seen again—and he had not even taken the penalties! Hibs were paired next with old rivals Renton in the semi-finals, and by winning 2–1, qualified to meet Hearts in the final. But like Vale of Leven in 1887, Renton tried to have the result annulled in the courts, alleging that one of the Hibs' full-backs had not been eligible to play.

They failed, however, and the final did take place, at Logie Green, then the home of St Bernards, and broadly where the Tesco supermarket at the western end of Beaverbank Road now stands. There was concern that the match might attract such a crowd that crushing would be a problem; the capacity was estimated at 22,000. In the event, these fears curtailed the actual attendance to only 16,000, at one shilling per head, and they saw Hearts win 3–1. The Gorgie team scored from a penalty in the first three minutes, and the writing appeared to be on the wall from that point. Willie Groves had returned to the fold from his trips to Glasgow and England, but although he was still a young man he was already affected by ill health. He had scored in the tie at Ibrox, but there was much soul searching as Hibs decided whether or not to play him in the final. In the event, Groves did play, but he had clearly lost much of the dash which had endeared him to the fans in the eighties, and he did not figure in team selection very much thereafter, before ending his career in England.

Logie Green did not feature much more in Edinburgh football, because a few years later, St Bernards were turfed out by their landlords, and moved to the Royal Gymnasium, a few hundred yards to the south-west, off Eyre Place. Hibs were still unhappy that their strange sloping pitch was not what a top club should have but attempts to move locally proved fruitless and in late 1902, it was reported that they had even thought about a move to Aberdeen, then without a top class side. Indeed, it was the threat of Hibs moving north which proved the catalyst for three local sides to team up to form the present

The *Edinburgh Evening Dispatch*'s artist's impression of the Logie Green cup final

Aberdeen F.C. Leith Athletic, whose history was one of nomadism, had moved to Beechwood Park, before returning to their previous home at Hawkhill, close to Easter Road. Even Hearts were thinking of moving and were soon negotiating with the Caledonian Railway Company to buy Meggetland. Given recent events, one wonders what the residents of Craiglockhart would have made of that!

During the next few years Hibs and Hearts remained the main challengers to the Old Firm. In 1896–97 Celtic had to play Hibs minus some of their stars who refused to play unless the press were excluded, following some newspaper criticism. On the final day of the same season, Hearts took the title only because Celtic lost at Dundee. Readers may notice a similarity here to 1986. Hibs finished third, had a 100% home record for the only time, and they had three players, Breslin, Kennedy and Murray, in the same Scottish team, for the first time, against Wales. The following year saw Rangers' completion of their league campaign without dropping a point, although their last-minute penalty goal at Easter Road, awarded by a referee who had previously played for Hearts, threatened to prove a serious health hazard for the official.

By now, Hibs were in a transitional phase. Allan Martin, who had returned from Celtic after only a year at Parkhead, retired through injury. His place went to Hamilton Handling, who, like his predecessor, could play in attack or defence, (but apparently not in goal). Paddy Callaghan from Jordanhill started a long career at inside forward, with Bobby Atherton on the left. Atherton was important because when Joe Baker was capped for England about sixty years later, Hibs were the then only Scottish club to have players capped by all four home associations. Bob Glen of Renton's 1895 cup final side was a major signing who added much solidity to the defence.

Harry Rennie

Beyond doubt Hibs biggest signing scoop was Harry G. Rennie, Hearts' international goalkeeper. Celtic had arranged his transfer, but when the negotiations hit a snag and Rennie was momentarily a free agent, Hibs stepped in. There were rumours about illegal payments, while Hibs claimed they were only giving him back pay for the close season, and the matter was referred to the International Board for a ruling. There turned out to be no precedent and the relevant wording was far from exact, so Hibs were cleared and Rennie was to be Hibs' goalkeeper for most of the next decade. He was years ahead of his time; he had a style all his own, keeping goal from the halfway line (when his own side was attacking, that was), and he drew up his own contract and presented it for Hibs to sign. Rennie's appearance was curiously lop-sided, apparently because of an unequal meeting with a cricket ball. He later had an operation to correct his appearance, but apparently it affected his eyesight and he was never quite as good afterwards.

Rennie's first season at Easter Road was 1900–01, a more momentous season for Hearts than Hibs; the Tynecastle men had to apply for re-election to the First Division, but bounced back to win the Scottish Cup. Practically the same thing happened to Hibs one year later. They scored only six league wins, and finished level on points with Queens Park, who were third from bottom. Then they too won the Cup.

The early ties were against Clyde then Port Glasgow Athletic and Queens Park, then the semi-final paired Hibs and Rangers, again in Glasgow. Again Hibs triumphed, this time by 2–0, but at the cost of a broken leg to their bustling right winger McCartney, shortly after he had scored the second goal. The final was against Celtic. To prove that there was no favouritism, the venue was Parkhead.

The 1902 Cup Final

The preparations were somewhat different to those today. After training, the Hibs players were kept in the Easter Road pavilion until after the pubs had closed, their mental and physical condition being kept at peak levels by never-ending games of dominoes and table tennis, hot chocolate and potted heid sandwiches by the score. At least it made sure they were looking forward to cup-final day!

When it came, cup-final day was dominated by the gale which swept Parkhead. Hibs were mostly on the receiving end during the first half, but with the defenders covering every approach to goal, Rennie was troubled only by longer range efforts. By the interval, the wind seemed even stronger, but the closest thing so far came when in a sudden break, Livingstone beat Rennie but the ball came back off a

Hibs' championship winning team of 1902–03

post. Against that, Atherton has what looked a valid goal disallowed, and so it was still all square when Callaghan took a corner with fifteen minutes remaining. Celtic full-back Battles seemed to leave the ball, and Andy McGeechan collected it, wheeled away from goal and cheekily backheeled the ball into the net. Rumours were rife that the goalscorer's repertoire of skills had extended to imitating the Irish brogue of the goalkeeper to deceive Battles, but the goal stood, and Hibs had won the trophy for the second time.

The trophy was presented to club president Phil Farmer in the Alexandria Hotel, and the party set off for the real celebrations in Edinburgh. 'The Scottish Referee', reported that 'it was strange that the Hibernians' victory was so universally popular', and that 'there were high jinks in Edinburgh when the Hibernians' special arrived. The rejoicing after Hearts' victory last year were not in it'. Soon afterwards, Hibs returned to Parkhead to beat Celtic 6–2, with a hat-trick by McGeechan, in the Glasgow Charity Cup final.

Champions

Hibs' run of success extended into the autumn of 1902. Dundee set the early pace in the First Division, and Hibs needed to win a vital game against Rangers on the Edinburgh September holiday just to stay in touch. Then came the crunch game against the Taysiders at Easter Road. McCartney, back from injury, scored the only goal, in a match which was the turning point of the whole campaign. Hibs went on to important wins at Ibrox and at Dens, while Dundee also lost against St Mirren and Hearts. Hibs' only reverse of the campaign came at Cathkin and their double over Rangers was the last for more than sixty years. With their rivals all taking points from one another, Hibs had twenty-one points by the end of October, followed by Rangers, Celtic, Dundee and Hearts all on thirteen. Their winning margin was nearly as great, as Hibs finished six points ahead of Dundee. It was the only time so far that Hibs have held the league trophy and the Scottish Cup at the same time.

— 4 —
STAYING PUT

The year 1903 was a time of change for Hibs. Their move to Aberdeen had fallen through, so that for the time being they had to make the most of what they had at Easter Road. In addition, they joined a growing trend and made the club a limited liability company. One aspect of that was that club matters were dealt with by a Board of Directors, and team selection, nominally at least by the team manager. Dan McMichael was the first Hibs' manager, a position he held until his death about the end of the Great War.

One reason for the change to company status was that Hibs would find it easier to raise finance to get the facilities a top club needed because their efforts to achieve them otherwise had not borne fruit. Unfortunately, the way that the problem was resolved in the short term was that Hibs quickly lost their top team tag. Among those that went south were Atherton, to Middlesborough, McGeechan, to Bradford and Robertson, to Manchester United, and Hibs attained complete mediocrity as early as their opening league defeat at Port Glasgow. It was to be a few years before the crowds attending Easter Road exceeded what the ground could take.

The First Division expanded to fourteen, sixteen and finally eighteen clubs during the first decade of the century, which meant that the league campaign continued into the new year rather than finishing about Christmas as before. It also meant that there was more to the second half of the season than a good cup run, which for Hibs was just as well, because they did not enjoy any more success there than in the league.

Goalscoring was the main problem, and Hibs were amongst the lowest scorers in the division, although, with almost exactly a point per game, their league position was average. Goals were not in great supply anyway, now that teams were playing two full backs and three

Harry G. Rennie, a unique goalkeeper

half-backs, because the off-side law required three defenders to be between the player receiving the ball and the opposing goal. This rule was not changed until the mid-1920s.

Various players were brought in to boost the goals rate; Peggie from East Fife and Duguid from Albion Rovers were two, but the most successful was Dick Harker. He was a former Crystal Palace player who scored a half century of goals for Hibs, but then went across the city to Hearts. Duguid had an interesting debut, playing under the clever alias of Smith because his clearance to play was outstanding. Opponents Hearts rumbled this imaginative ploy, and Hibs had to forfeit the hard-earned points. There was also the lure of greater earnings in England, which was why winger George Smith, who was capped while still with Hibs, and captain and centre-half McConnachie were lost to Hibs. Then in 1908, Harry Rennie went to Rangers, to be replaced by Willie Allan, from Falkirk.

By 1908–09 however, Hibs had signed a number of players who were to give sterling service, in particular Willie Smith, a clever and nippy winger with a penchant for the spectacular, Mattha Paterson, who captained the side from centre-half, and more than once filled in at centre-forward when the drought of goals became critical, and James Main, who was capped at right-back early in his career. Willie Smith's career was a long one, and had an amusing climax when, well into his thirties, he was 'spotted' by an English scout and invited south for a week's trial; it was only when he got there that his age and pedigree became known to his hosts, but Willie stayed on to enjoy the holiday at their expense.

A Year to Remember

The year 1909 stands out from the ordinary during this period, for a number of reasons. Harry Rennie would remember it because, with Rangers, he played in the cup final which was abandoned and the trophy withheld following a riot at Hampden. The Irish community in Dundee would remember it, as they formed their own club, Dundee Hibernians, now Dundee United, to copy Hibs. The Edinburgh originals hanselled their new ground, Tannadice, in August, and had to play in Leith Athletic's black and white hoops to avoid a colour clash.

Left. The Wilson New Year Cup—played for in the first Hibs–Hearts New Year Derby. Presented 1905. (courtesy HFC Museum)
Right. Tom Hart Memorial Trophy (courtesy of HFC Museum)

Colour clashes were not taken to the extremes they are now, and the idea of several reproduction strips to extract ever-increasing sums of from supporters and their parents was not yet the norm, so that Hibs had not had a change strip up to that point. The score was 1–1, and Hibs' O'Hara was presented with a bicycle by Dundee's Lord Provost for scoring the first goal at the new ground.

1909 was also the year in which Hibs grand plans to build a grand new stadium foundered. It had been constructed at Piershill, a mile from Easter Road and roughly where the Miller-built Mountcastle estate now stands, and was equipped with a cycle and running track, as well as space for fifty thousand spectators. The whole project was virtually complete, when the North British Railway Company obtained a court order to build a railway line through a corner of the site. The line was never actually built, and the stadium was used for minor cup finals and the like for many years, but Hibs were prevented from moving. With the prospect of moving to Piershill, of course, little maintenance had taken place at Easter Road, which by now had a truly dilapidated aspect.

Finally, on Christmas Day 1909, James Main, Hibs still only twenty-three, was carried off at Firhill playing against Partick Thistle, and died a few days later from internal injuries. Main had already been capped by Scotland, and was the outstanding prospect in the team. His replacement was Peter Kerr, from East Lothian, but Hibs were hard pressed to acquire his services, especially after his mother found out why Hibs needed a replacement!

Meanwhile, Hibs continued on their unexceptional path in the middle of the First Division, right up until the First World War interrupted the proceedings. The goal drought continued, and fact reached new depths in 1909–10. Hibs managed only thirty-three goals in thirty-four games, and no one player scoring more than five. The nearest to that in recent times was in 1982–83, when Rae, Murray and Thompson shared the lead with six goals, in thirty-six games. Highlights were few. Paterson would need no reminding of the game at Ibrox in 1911–12, when he conceded a penalty in three minutes to gift Rangers their first goal, was carried off after having his face smashed in a collision with Chapman, and returned to the fray only to carried off with a further head knock—after only fifteen minutes. A young centre called Bell came into the 'famous for fifteen minutes' category

Back Row: P. CANNON (*Trainer*). J. WEIR. C. ALLAN. W. R. ALLAN. T. A. BIRRELL. WM. SMITH. J. H. SHARP.
Middle Row: J. MAIN. ... MAIN. P. ... RSON. WM. DUGUID. J. PEGGIE. D. CALLAGHAN.
Front ... JOHN O'HARA. [*Photo by Agnew & Son, Glasg...*]

The Hibs team of about 1909

as he scored the last two goals in the return fixture at Easter Road—a real upset this as Hibs, well under strength, beat the champions 5–0. On the other hand, Hibs lost nine of their ten league games against Hearts in 1909–14.

Another Cup Final

They had more success against the men from Gorgie in the cup, though, and not without a touch of the farce which had attended some of their meetings in the early days. The first cup pairing for a few years took place in 1909–10, and showed Easter Road in a very poor light. The crowd was twenty-seven thousand and the ground could not take it. Easter Road was bursting at the seams, and what with the insecure footing on the bankings which surrounded much of the pitch and the underfoot conditions, the wooden palings at the front were breached continually during the second half as the crowd tried good-humouredly to see the game to a close. Things went from bad to worse, and the tie was brought to an abrupt stop after sixty-five minutes, with Hearts leading 1–0. The clubs agreed to count it as a draw and arranged the replay for Tynecastle. The SFA rather out of character agreed to this commonsense solution, and to the further surprise of many Peggie scored the only goal in a well-deserved Hibs win.

Two years on, and the teams were drawn together again, this time at Tynecastle, and a fiercely contested goalless draw was the outcome. The replay at Easter Road was played in the most dreadful conditions of sleet and snow, which completely obliterated the lines. Because of the conditions, the two clubs agreed to count the game as a friendly, but the crowd and press were only told about that after the game, after everyone had been charged the full admission price. The referee's report mentioned that he had instructed the teams to clear the lines, but they had not done so. Officialdom was not best pleased at this, as it infringed whatever of their rules was relevant, and fined both clubs £25, as well as the referee a guinea for not having abandoned the game when his orders were ignored. Hearts were indignant, having taken the reasonable view that it was not up to them to make Easter Road playable, and only paid up some weeks later under threat of suspension.

The first replay was therefore replayed at Easter Road, and resulted in the same score, 1–1. Both clubs wanted to toss for venue for the third game, but the SFA had clearly had enough of them, and sent them to settle the matter at Ibrox, where Hearts won by 3–1.

The final that Hibs reached in 1914 was to be the last before the war, and to get there, Hibs had to account for, among others, Rangers. A crowd of thirty thousand, another record, crowded into Easter Road for this one, so things must have been quite tight, although ground conditions were at least better. That Rangers held only a one goal advantage playing with the wind was down above all to Willie Allan in goal, and soon after the interval, Hendren equalised. The tempo and tension grew as the final whistle approached, and the game boiled over when Smith scored Hibs' winner from a corner.

It was a win that gave Hibs a lot of heart. They had by now the makings of a sound team, and it was unfortunate that they had so little time together before the war split them apart. Jimmy Hendren had been signed from Cowdenbeath during 1911–12 season, and after taking a few months to settle in the top league, proved a valuable goalscorer, with over fifty league goals alone in three seasons to 1915. Other new faces included Bobby Templeton, a left-back from Neilston

Victoria, and to be a future manager, the irrepressible Sam Fleming, at outside-right or inside forward, Peter Kerr, who had developed into a first class wing-half, and Sandy Grosart, at left half. In addition, Allan, Paterson, Smith and Callaghan remained from the old guard. They were all at Ibrox for the 1914 cup final against Celtic.

It was Willie Smith who remembered the first game longest; the score was 0–0, the game hard fought, and in the closing minutes the Hibs' left-winger, with just the goalkeeper to beat, had a miss which haunted him for the rest of his days. The replay took place the following Thursday, and lasted as a contest just eleven minutes. By that time, Celtic's new young centre Jimmy McColl had taken two chances to put the game beyond Hibs. Brownlee added two more before Smith scored a consolation for Hibs.

The First World War

The First World War kicked off in Sarajevo in the autumn of 1914, with a mood of optimism at least in the UK. Expectations were high that a prolonged conflict was impossible with the sophisticated weaponry now available—although cavalry was still very much in evidence too—and volunteers were urged to enlist in order to get a bit of the action before it was all over.

The Scottish football season had started before the hostilities on the continent, and the First Division continued despite them, although the Scottish Cup competition was in abeyance during the war. This was to comply with a War Office request, so that football would not interfere with recruitment for the army. Why this should apply to cup matches and not league games remains a mystery.

The story of wartime football was that the natural advantages of the clubs in the west were enhanced. Apart from the bigger population, Clydeside's heavy industries meant that many of the players of these clubs were in jobs which were considered vital to the war effort while enlistment was voluntary, and thereby exempt from conscription when that was introduced in 1916. Clubs in the east had a difficult time during the war, and Hibs were no exception.

League football in England was regionalised, but the Scottish First Division remained as one, although from 1915, the Second Division was split into Western and Eastern Leagues, each of twelve clubs. After

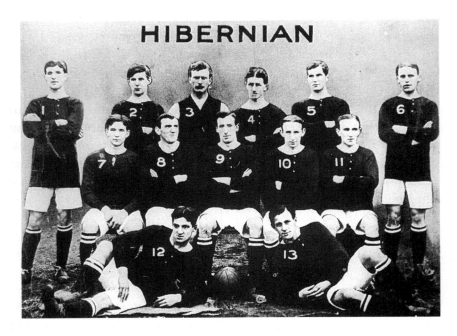

Hibs pictured around the start of World War 1

only one year, the Eastern League was reduced to ten, and the following year to seven, despite the addition of Aberdeen, Dundee and Raith Rovers, all of whom had resigned from the First Division without any guarantee of re-admission. It was no surprise that Clydebank F.C., who came from a town which at that time had more men employed in shipbuilding than on the unemployment register, were able to take up one vacant spot in the top league to even up the numbers. One further year later, the Eastern League had closed down altogether.

Hibs' deteriorating fortunes gave a good example of the more general difficulties. In 1914–15 they finished eleventh of twenty. By 1915 three million men were in uniform, and only those in full-time employment were allowed to play football, following press criticism of the decision to continue the leagues. Many first team regulars were missing; many more went when conscription was brought in, and as though that was not bad enough, Hibs' right winger Alexander had an arm amputated after an accident at work. By 1917–18, women were put in most male jobs at home, to let even more men go to the war, and Hibs finished fourth bottom. By 1918–19, Field Marshall Haig was told that the current offensive had to be the decisive one because there was no-one left to send to Flanders.

By now, Hibs and Hearts were the only two out of seventeen eastern clubs still in action who were playing just three years earlier. Hibs fielded thirty-five players during the season, and even then were not always able to field eleven on a Saturday. Full-back Bobby Templeton often had to turnout in goal, and for a Wilson Cup-tie against Hibs, Hearts had to recruit a goalkeeper from the crowd. Small wonder that a lightweight Hibs team were taken apart to the tune of 9–2 in the Cappielow glaur—Greenock then had a connection with shipbuilding too.

All was not gloom, however. Thanks mainly to the tireless Dan McMichael, the club did keep going, and indeed of the many youngsters tried, quite a few made the side which brought Hibs comparative success in the post-war period; Miller, Dornan, McGinnigle and Hugh Shaw, then a centre with Clydebank Juniors, all made wartime appearances, while others formed the nucleus of the reserve side which was started in 1919. Unfortunately, McMichael, who had been with Hibs since their rebirth in 1892, died in the 'flu epidemic of 1919, to be replaced as manager by Davy Gordon, an ex-Hull City player who had also guested for Hibs during the war.

The Victory Cup

After the armistice, players came trickling back, and the first home were in time to be involved in a Victory Cup competition. Twenty-eight sides took part, all those still in the First Division plus eight others from Coatbridge westwards. Hibs reached the semi-finals, but lost 3–1 to the eventual winners St. Mirren. The cup run was important because things had been so desperate during the war that Hibs' only set of green jerseys were by now yellow with the sweat of many players over many seasons, while the white goalkeeper's jersey was a dirty grey. This was before the advent of Ariel Ultra. Prices had doubled from the pre-war days, to one shilling, but although the cup proceeds went to provide a new strip, there was little left to give Easter Road even the most basic facelift.

The Twenties

When peacetime football was resumed in season 1919–20, the First Division was as big as it was to get, with twenty-two teams, which meant forty-two league games, a number only exceeded in some of the sillier seasons in the Premier League. There was therefore no time for many of the local competitions which had previously taken up the final weeks of the season. Under the top division there were three regional leagues, western, eastern and central. The Central League was the strongest, and with some Western League teams made up the new Second Division when automatic promotion and relegation was eventually introduced in 1921–22.

Since Hibs had hardly been a top side before hostilities or during them, it was to their credit that within a few months *The Scotsman* noted that they were 'developing into a capital team'. They were to cruise along in the top half of the league for most of the next few years, and finish third in 1924–25, their only top three finish between 1903 and 1948. Certainly there were a few mishaps on the way, such as losing seven goals at both Parkhead and Ibrox in that first season, but the team were largely forgiven by the fans by beating Hearts at New Year. That was a curious game because the Tynecastle team scored three of the four goals. Despite their comparative, to Hibs, success during the war, this was the start of a difficult period for Hearts, and in 1921–22, Hibs beat them five times out of five.

Much of the team had already begun to take shape, McGinnigle and Dornan had already formed a sound full-back partnership, and the brawny Hugh Shaw had been converted into a formidable left-half noted for exacting retribution on behalf of less physically endowed colleagues who had been abused by opponents. Peter Kerr continued a long career at right-half, and was eventually rewarded with a League cap. Up front, Harry Ritchie, a strong bustling winger who could cut in from either touchline to have a shot at goal, had become a crowd favourite, and, much like Arthur Duncan later, was forgiven many a slip as a result.

The remaining pieces of the jigsaw fell into place in due course. It was in September 1920 that both Jimmy Dunn and Willie Harper made their debuts against Airdrie. Dunn was a typical tricky Scottish inside forward, signed from St Anthony's, and later was one of the famous

Wembley Wizards. Harper was a blacksmith from Winchburgh in West Lothian, and had been a boxing champion in the forces among many other sporting achievements apart from being the best goal-keeper of his time. He was signed from Edinburgh Emmett, who played at what became the New Street bus station off the High Street, and played for Scotland against England four times, without being on the losing side.

Johnny Halligan had joined Hibs from Glasgow junior football, and when 'Darkie' Walker was signed from Kirkintilloch Rob Roy, they formed a left-wing partnership, with Ritchie partnering Dunn on the right. In the centre, Hibs signed Jimmy McColl, who had moved from Celtic to Stoke but had not settled in the Potteries. McColl stayed with Hibs in various roles for the next half century.

This Hibs team was to become noted more for their cup exploits than their satisfactory league performances, but their cup runs did not get off to the best of starts when the competition resumed in 1919–20. Their first tie was against Galston, on a bog of a pitch which, to make matters worse, had been subject to subsidence. A goalless draw was a relief, and the Ayrshire team were no pushovers in the replay at Easter Road either, with a tight match ending 2–1.

The reward for this effort was a trip to Armadale, where Hibs lost by the only goal. Armadale had Willie Robb in goal, later to play for both Hibs and Scotland, and were on their best ever run as giant-killers, the term being only used in the comparative sense however since their other scalps were Ayr United and Clyde. Albion Rovers were the real giant-killers, and having done the hard bit by beating Rangers after three games in the semi-finals, lost to Partick Thistle at the last hurdle.

The 1921 and 1922 competitions was no better for Hibs, with second round exits to Motherwell and Partick Thistle, but in 1923 Hibs at last made a breakthrough. It was also a tournament which brought many upsets, especially in the second round. Hibs themselves had a close call with a goalless draw against Peebles Rovers, but won through at the second time of asking. Hearts meanwhile lost at Bo'ness, Rangers went out at Ayr and Dundee Hibs lost at home to Nithsdale Wanderers from Sanquhar.

Hibs' next cup victories were against Queens Park and Aberdeen, which brought them to the semi-final stage. Their opponents were

Third Lanark, and the venue Tynecastle. The game was poor but Dunn scored the only goal, by forcing the goalkeeper into an error. The final was diappointingly similar. Hibs lost 1–0 to Celtic at Hampden, and the goal was credited to Cassidy, helped by a rare error by Harper.

The most enduring memory of the 1924 campaign was not the final, which Hibs reached, but the tie at Ibrox on the way to it. The early ties should have been straightforward, against Alloa and Dundee United, but it took two games to dispose of the former. The crowd at Ibrox for the third round tie was 53,000, and Hibs' success was the more remarkable because Rangers led at the interval. They had most of the second-half play too, but goals by Walker and Murray, a makeshift centre in McColl's absence, sent Hibs home happy.

It was still to be a long road to the final. It took Hibs three games to get the better of Partick Thistle, and then in the semi-finals, Walker scored the only goal late on in five hours of travail against Aberdeen. The final was a big let-down. Airdrie provided the opposition, and scored in two minutes, and again before half-time to win comfortably. Hibs had gambled on Dunn's fitness, and more than a little sentiment came into the decision to field the same eleven as a year earlier. The gamble failed, Dunn and Ritchie had to switch places, and the potential threat from Hibs' right wing was blunted.

Much was happening off the field too in 1924, because during the summer Hibs ground was completely rebuilt.

— 5 —

THE THIRD EASTER ROAD

The decision to redevelop Easter Road, and finally, or so it seemed at the time, abandon any plans to move elsewhere, had been taken during the 1922–23 season. The two main reasons were much the same as seventy years later—a suitable site had not been found, and the fact that the support was mainly local, and between the time and expense, it was doubtful how many would travel to watch home matches, especially if the team was not playing well.

Another consideration was that Hibs' lease on Easter Road expired in 1925, and therefore a new one had to be negotiated. The terms this time were for another twenty-five years, at £250 per annum. Plans and planning consent were the next hurdles, so that the actual construction did not take place until the close season of 1924.

By this time, Albion Road and Albion Place has been built, the latter so far a cul-de-sac which extended only as far as the present entrance to the North Stand; the corner of Hibs' old ground had been a barrier to its going further. The plan was to extend Albion Road beyond the St Andrew's Steelworks, then at right angles past an aereated water factory to link up with an extended Albion Place to the north-east of the ground, on what is now Hawkhill Avenue. (This part of the development, and the aerated water plant, was superseded by the later extension of the terracing to increase the capacity to the requirements of post-1945 crowds). The pitch was moved some yards to the east, so that the new grandstand, to seat 4480 persons, could be built on the west side, to spare those inside the problems of sun, wind and rain to which the old west-facing stand had left them exposed. Most of the extra room needed was acquired by demolishing some old buildings which had been behind the old west terracing, but space was limited at the north-east corner by the church hall in Albion Place, and the school playground behind the stand.

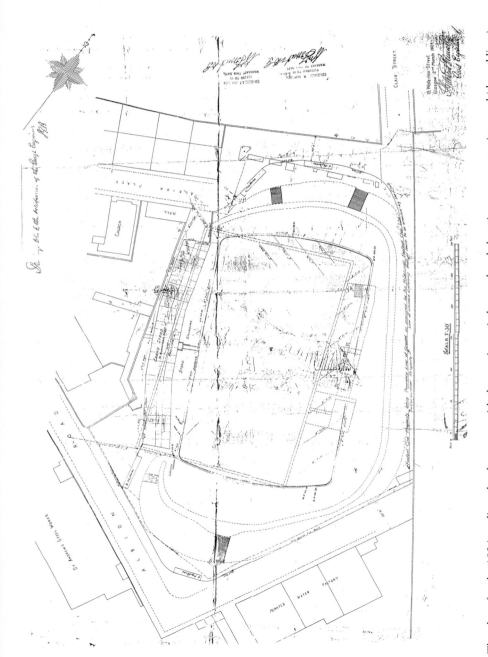

The plans for the 1924 stadium development, with the previous pitch, stand and changing rooms superimposed (dotted lines)

The terracing round three sides of the ground was designed to bring the capacity of the stadium to 45,000, and those at the top of the terracing, along with those in passing aircraft would be able to see the giant Father Time logo of Scottish Brewers which was later painted on the grandstand roof. Entrances were at each end of the ground, (as well as the present entrances to the stand and enclosure), with steps leading from the top of the terracing at the south end directly on to Albion Road and from the north end on to Albion Place.

The cost was high, about £20,000. The present-day equivalent, as measured by the RPI, would be £500,000, but in terms of inflation as measured by terracing admission charges, say one shilling in 1925 and £8 now, would be £3,200,000, or of the same order as the present project to build stands at each end of the pitch. The money was raised mainly from debenture issues, as well as the sale of their goalkeeper Harper to Arsenal in 1925. As recent a publication as the 1924 Cup Final programme had noted that compared to other football clubs, Hibs remained 'a close and private concern' and so the debenture issue, bringing the existing board into contact with businessmen whose concerns would be based on finance rather than sentiment was good for the club, and was certainly to shape its future.

To complete the work on schedule was a daunting task, and a strike by the construction workers prevented its success. When the work was not completed when season 1924–25 kicked off, therefore, Hibs had to borrow Tynecastle for their opening league games, and to play on Friday evenings because St Bernards were in a similar position, and had arranged to use Hearts' ground on alternate Saturdays.

Hibs only had to play two home games at Tynecastle, beating Partick Thistle and Motherwell, before their new home was ready. Queens Park were the visitors on a festive occasion, and, with Ritchie outstanding on the right wing, Hibs won by two goals to nil. In fact, they topped the league at one point in October, and again briefly in March, but on the second occasion, Rangers and Airdrie, the country's top two at the time, had games in hand, because of having gone further in the cup. Both sides picked up enough points in these games to overhaul Hibs, who finished third.

Another important decision had been taken in season in 1922–23, that of scrapping a reserve team to save money. History has often shown that the cutting back on investment is often false economy in anything but the shortest term, and so it proved with Hibs. The decision was made during Alex Maley's spell as manager. He had taken over from Davy Gordon, and is often credited with the comparative success of his predecessor, apart from which he was widely disliked and mistrusted because of his links with Celtic, and in particular, some of the defectors of 1888. But in 1925, Maley too was replaced. Hibs hoped to attract the Clyde manager Paddy Travers, but when that idea foundered, the choice lay between Bob Templeton and Peter Kerr. Templeton got the job, and soon afterwards Kerr went to Hearts. A reserve team was started again around that time, but by then there was a dispute between the Glasgow junior sides, where Hibs tended to get a lot of their players, and the senior sides about compensation, and with only the rest of the country to choose from, Hibs' recruitment suffered.

For season 1925–26, the laws of the game were altered, so that only two rather than three defenders were needed to prevent offside. This increased the number of goals scored by about a third in the league as a whole, and it is no coincidence that many of the game's scoring records were established while the new rule was still new. Hibs' contribution to the goal orgy started by losing 5–0 at Celtic Park. There was much confusion about the interpretation of the rule, and some in the Hibs' camp claimed that not one of the five goals should have stood. The referee did not seem too sure about some aspects, and was seen consulting his rule book at the interval, although my understanding was that just one word in the rules had changed!

Following the defeat at Parkhead, Hibs' results did not improve much, especially at Aberdeen, where, with only Miller of the usual defence because of a catalogue of injuries, Hibs lost again by the same score. Harper was one of those sidelined, although he sometimes played while quite lame. On other occasions, manager Templeton deputised for Harper. When he was fit again, he played only one game before being transferred to Arsenal for £5,000, a world record for a goalkeeper. By November, Hibs had slipped to bottom of the league.

The second half of the season was better than the first, but not a lot. One highlight was the coming from behind three times to draw 4–4 against Celtic, but at the other end of the scale, Hibs missed three penalties in losing to Cowdenbeath. Hibs finally exorcised the spectre of relegation with a fortunate goal at Clydebank scored by Hugh Shaw.

The tale of the late twenties was one of the team being run down without the club having the money to provide equivalent replacements. Certainly, for 1926–27 Hibs signed a top class goalkeeper, Willie Robb from Rangers, who had been instrumental in Hibs cup defeat at Armadale some years earlier, but at the expense of Hugh Shaw's going to Ibrox. With Kerr having left, Dick from Airdrie and Gilfinnan from Celtic were brought in at wing-half. Walker on the left lost his place to Bradley, from St Roch's. The results were erratic, with a league double against Hearts and two draws against Celtic, but with defeats from four of the five bottom sides, Hibs finished six places down at ninth.

The next season produced a reasonable, and by now rare, cup run, culminating in a semi-final against Rangers at Tynecastle. Obviously the rules about Rangers playing more than five miles from Ibrox have changed since then. Since Rangers had lost at Easter Road a week earlier, the crowd of 44,000 expected more than the one-sided encounter they saw, ending in a 3–0 win for Rangers. The league performances showed further slippage, twelfth position to be exact, but there promising signs. Robb was capped against Wales, Ritchie and Dunn against Ireland, and Dunn became a Wembley Wizard in the famous 5–1 win against England. In addition, McColl and Dunn became the first two players to reach a hundred league and cup goals for Hibs. The downside was that Dunn, with Ritchie, were transferred to Everton in 1928, to be replaced by Finlay, who had signed from Dundee United a couple of years earlier without making a great impression, and the veteran utility man Geordie Murray.

In addition, full-backs McGinnigle and Dornan and centre-half Miller retired, to be replaced by Hector Wilkinson and Bertie Stark and Dick respectively. McColl and Halligan were showing their years more too, and Hibs slipped further to fourteenth. Hibs were heading towards danger, and by the following new year, they were in the centre of their first relegation dog-fight, with only a single point covering Hibs, Airdrie, Dundee United and St Johnstone at the foot of the table. Airdrie were the first to get themselves out of danger, before an unbeaten run of seven games from Hibs meant there was no escape for the Tayside rivals.

The Scotsman thought nevertheless that Hibs were 'a team of distinct possibilities', but the basis for this optimism was not clear to many. The most promising move was the signing of Duncan Urquhart, a rugged full-back from Galloway. Robb had broken his finger and lost his place to George Blyth, and 'Ginger' Watson came in at centre-half, to give the defence a more settled and firm look. But Hibs difficulties up front were chronic. McCall and Halligan were by now only turning out occasionally. Ritchie had not been replaced effectively, but although he had been unsettled with Everton and wanted back to Scotland, it was Dundee and not Hibs who could afford him. And so a year later, the distinct possibility which became a reality was relegation.

Even while still a struggling First Division side, however, there was cause for concern. 1930 was in the aftermath of the Wall Street crash, which was followed by a worldwide slump. Unemployment was high, and among the less serious consequences, attendances at football matches suffered. On many occasions, the total gate receipts were less than the guarantee, or minimum sum, which was the away team's share of the gate. Some clubs let the unemployed in free, but that did not do much for the finances. Many clubs found themselves in trouble, and even Manchester United went into receivership and could not raise the £150 asking price for the transfer of Matt Busby. It was at this time that Clyde introduced dog-racing to Shawfield to help pay the bills. Some clubs did eventually go to the wall, notably Arthurlie, Bo'ness and Armadale, all of the Second Division. In the First Division, Leith Athletic also went out of business, but performed one of these overnight structural re-incarnations to allow them to fulfil the fixtures, failure of which to do meant expulsion from the league.

Hibs creditors, the debenture holders, were not satisfied to have their assets managed without their involvement, especially with the downward trend since 1925 in the club's fortunes seemingly unchecked, and argued for and eventually got representation on the board of directors. In particular, the elderly Pat Smith agreed to transfer his shares to this group and Harry Swan and Tom Hartland came on to the board. Alex Maley completed the new look, and Owen Brannigan, although even older than Smith, became chairman. It was a major departure for the club, because although it had been a limited liability company since 1903, and non-sectarian in the playing sense since 1892, the reins had always been held by the small all-Catholic group whose relatives had been involved since the previous century, a situation which was maintained with share transfers requiring the approval of the board.

One way of looking after their interests was to help the club avoid relegation, and so the new board soon authorised the funds necessary to bring the Irish internationalist right-half Joe Miller from Middlesbro' and 'Brick' Wallace from Burnley. Sadly neither made a great impact, and were out of the team as often as in it. Hibs were still as far away as ever from having a forward line worthy of the name, and even centre-half Dick was tried there. Easily the brightest prospect was Watson, a centre-half from Stoneyburn Juniors, whose rapid progress enabled Hibs to deploy Dick elsewhere.

Early results were not encouraging, but Hibs managed to keep their noses in front of East Fife and Ayr United. By New Year they were five points ahead of the Somerset side, but with two more games played. The Cup brought some relief, and a couple of noteworthy events, even if it only lasted until the third round. The first was that in an unmemorable 3–1 win against St Cuthbert's Wanderers, the Saints' goalscorer was called Pagan; the second was that the third round tie against Motherwell brought a record attendance of 33,300 to Easter Road. The Hibs' support was roused for a big effort after McColl had scored four in a replay against Hamilton in the previous round, and were disappointed firstly when McColl was not playing, and then when Motherwell cruised to a 3–0 win.

So it was back to the misery of the league. The same three were the candidates for the drop as at the turn of the year, and Hibs did their chances no good by losing 1–0 away to the doomed East Fife, even if Hearts did score nine against Ayr on the same afternoon.

When Hibs had five games to go, they had six points more, and a better goal average, than Ayr who had three more games remaining, so that the chances seemed that they would escape. But Hibs managed only one win more, so that after their last game, the points difference had vanished, and Hibs were ahead of Ayr only on goal average. Unfortunately Ayr still had a game at home against Kilmarnock to come, they won it 1–0, and Hibs went down with East Fife. Among others, the debenture holders were still not very happy.

The Second Division

It did not take Hibs long to experience the grimness of life in the Second Division. Despite losing few players, a hard-earned single goal victory against Alloa was followed by defeats by St Bernards and Forfar in the first week, and their regular attendance quickly halved to around four thousand. There was a brief flurry of hope with six goal performances against St. Johnstone, one of the best teams in the division, and Dunfermline, but little else. Edinburgh City, an amateur side in their first season in the league, achieved their first ever league win against Hibs, and goalkeeper Blyth broke his leg in another derby defeat by St Bernards. Without any consistency, Hibs finished with little over a point a game, and lost their first tie in the Scottish Cup as well as every local competition.

However one viewed it, it was a disastrous season. Finishing seventh in the Second Division meant being twenty-seventh in the country. Hearts and Leith were in the First Division and St Bernards finished two places above Hibs, so the Easter Road side was only fourth in Edinburgh. And they were below such giants as East Stirlingshire, who were champions, Forfar Athletic and Stenhousemuir.

A year later, it was all so different. Hibs had four new players, all forwards, who made a big difference, and of whom Peter Flucker and Rab Walls made the grade and gave good First Division service too. Hibs won fifteen out of the opening eighteen league matches, and seemed uncatchable.

There were a couple of oddities during the second half of the season. The first was that Hibs clinched the championship twice. The first time was on March 25th, with a 4–1 win against St Bernards. Then the League decided to expunge the records of Bo'ness and Armadale, who had failed to meet their financial commitments. Since Hibs had taken six points in their three games against these unfortunates, their lead over the pack was cut, and it was not until they beat Dumbarton 1–0 three weeks later that they could again claim to be champions. The second was that in between these celebrations, Hibs lost to Stenhousemuir, their first league defeat of 1933. Since Stenhousemuir had beaten Hibs twice the previous season, this gave them a 75% record against Hibs, which is still intact and the highest of any league club.

There was also a further attendance record for Easter Road, though not by much. It was obvious that the Edinburgh fans missed the Hibs-Hearts derbies, although Hibs of course had just had six league derbies against Leith, St Bernards, and Edinburgh City. Hibs had beaten Aberdeen to reach the third round, with one of the very last goals from Johnny Halligan, so that when the pair were drawn against each other a crowd of 33,759 witnessed it. Despite the capacity of the ground being gradually extended throughout the thirties, that record stood until crowd restrictions were lifted after the 1939–45 war.

Harry Swan

It was also in 1933 that Harry Swan, easily the most dynamic member of the Hibs' board, became chairman, a position he was to hold for the next thirty years. In many ways Hibs seemed a strange choice for his attention, for although he was not overtly anti-Catholic at a time when that was a big political issue, especially in Leith, much of his effort was geared to moving the club's image away from its roots. Thus at various times, Swan was responsible for the curtailment of free entry for priests, or at least their prior booking, the unpublicised demolition of a wall at the main entrance bearing the harp crest, which was not there when the wall was rebuilt, and the suggestions that the club's name and colours be changed to make it more acceptable to the majority in the city who had no affiliation to the Emerald Isle. It was in 1938 that the white sleeves which Bert Herdman's great Arsenal side had made fashionable, were introduced to Hibs' green jerseys, and Swan wanted to go the whole hog and change the green to red too.

When he took over the chairmanship, Swan was quoted as saying that he would make Hibs great in ten years. His first job along with manager Templeton was the more mundane one of keeping them in the First Division, but at least they were able to kick off with a team of whom nearly all had some top league experience. Initiallly, Hibs performed acceptably at a point a game, but by Christmas they had drifted down near trouble. A positive sign was that centre-half Watson won a league cap and left-back Urquhart a full one. They signed Peter Kavanagh, the Celtic veteran, and the skilful if ponderous inside-forward John Smith from Hearts. A 5–4 win against Clyde after trailing 4–1 at the interval was a rare break from the struggle in the league, but Hibs survived. Their marketing effort did not seem to be in full swing—only a hundred people watched their last game at Dens, because Dundee United were playing Albion Rovers at Tannadice! Kavanagh and Wallace were among those freed.

In 1935–36. Hibs had a better season. A major signing in August was Peter Wilson, a popular internationalist wing-half from Celtic, and Hibs had more points than games by Christmas. They also scored their only win against the Parkhead side between 1928–29 and ten years later. A late lapse cost them their top half position, but Hibs finished eleventh, and the fact that the run-in was not vital to their survival was a pleasant change.

Any thoughts that Mr Swan had had that he was getting somewhere were soon dashed. Hibs managed only one win in eight starts in 1935–36 and suffered a climactic visit at Tynecastle. Hibs were swept aside, and were six goals down shortly after the interval when Hearts eased up and Hibs scored three goals in quick order. The home team got another two, and the embarrassment did not end there. Rumours were rife about the behaviour of two of the Hibs players, and the condition in which they turned up at Tynecastle. One of them had been physically unwell on the pitch before the game started. That there were grounds for these stories seemed to be confirmed when Watson and Urquhart, the only two club representatives honoured for years, were given free transfers, and went to Ayr and Aberdeen. It was a risky move, despite the circumstances, and Hibs finished 1935 in second bottom place, losing seven goals at Shawfield.

Harry Swan, a master baker, was not one of the modern breed of millionaire chairmen, and when he and his manager went to Belfast in December to sign the Irish internationalist centre-half Jack Jones from Linfield, as well as teammate William Gowdy, it was only because the transaction was funded by a sympathetic local bookmaker. But by February, the team had managed only one more win, against cup minnows Vale Acoba, and things were looking bleak. Manager Templeton resigned after twenty-five years with the club.

Johnny Halligan was made caretaker until the relegation issue was settled. Defeat at Dundee soon put Hibs bottom again. Hibs then borrowed Hearts' young goalkeeper Waugh, a future international, and left-back Munro. Waugh had an unfortunate error to gift Ayr the points in a crucial match which Hibs seemed to have control of, but redeemed himself with two penalties to give Hibs a single-goal win at Kilmarnock in the fourth last game. Hibs were able to beat Third Lanark, who had little at stake, but were denied an unlikely win at Motherwell by a late equaliser. That meant that they had to win at Dunfermline in the last game to survive.

A horde of Hibs supporters made the trip to Fife, not unlike the trip to Kirkcaldy in similar circumstances in 1963. The game was scrappy, but the only goal came from a huge leap by the diminutive centre Willie Black, who had come to Hibs three years earlier from Arthurlie. It turned out to be as important a goal as Hibs have scored.

— 6 —
WILLIE McCARTNEY

It was not only Hibs' important win at Dunfermline which was to be mirrored thirty years later, but the aftermath which was to change the club's fortunes. Just as Jock Stein was persuaded to come to Easter Road in 1964, a few days after Hibs guaranteed their survival in 1936 they announced a new manager, Willie McCartney. Like Stein, McCartney had already been a successful manager and commanded a lot of respect, although as manager of Hearts he had not won anything, and indeed he had been out of the game since he and the Tynecastle club parted about a year earlier. Swan and McCartney had been in contact during the season, but the latter had agreed to come only if Hibs stayed up.

Times had changed by the sixties of course, and the styles of McCartney and Stein could scarcely have differed more. There was no such thing as a tracksuit manager, there was no coaching to speak of, and there were no tactics, because nobody had questioned the accepted 2-3-5 formation. Training was the responsibility of the trainer. The manager's job, on the playing side was therefore to find the best players, and that was what Willie McCartney excelled at. Also, although he had never played at the top level, McCartney was held in respect by the players who had, and he was never averse to dropping any of his stars whom he had felt had let him down. More ample of girth than stature, McCartney had a booming voice and was never happier than when centre-stage, where he was seldom seen without bowler hat and buttonhole.

McCartney's first acts were to issue a list of free transfers which included Rab Walls of the first XI, and to bring Hugh Shaw in as trainer in place of Christie Henderson. For the new season, he signed Gourlay, a goalkeeper from Partick Thistle, and his clubmate Prior, a right-back. Winger Alex Ritchie and inside man Johnny McKay,

Left. Summer Cup 1964. (courtesy HFC Museum)
Right. Gift from Slavia Prague in 1946 Czechoslovakia tour. (courtesy HFC Museum)

whose only cap had come fourteen years earlier, were stop-gap measures. McCartney also tried to presuade Barney Battles out of retirement to help, but without success. Meanwhile Johnny Halligan went to scout for Sunderland.

A crowd of twenty-five thousand turned up for Hibs' difficult first match against Aberdeen. The Dons took the points, and fewer were turning out by the end of the first quarter by when Hibs were in familiar territory at second bottom. Peter Wilson had been discarded as too old, but he was recalled, and a better sequence of results meant that Hibs were fifth bottom at Christmas. The second half of the season was no better. A cup win against Alloa was one of only seven victories all season, five of them away from home, and Hibs finished fourth from bottom.

However, they were still in the First Division, and behind the scenes, McCartney was gathering an impressive array of youngsters. Tommy McIntyre, Portobello Renton's right winger, was an instant success, and earned a league cap before going to the war. Willie Finnegan, a tricky inside forward impressed with Bo'ness Cadora despite having to work on Saturday afternoons. Sammy Kean came from Rob Roy, and Jimmy Kerr, a brilliant young goalkeeper, from Ormiston Primrose. They were all just seventeen, Taysider Charlie Birse came in at wing-half, so that Tommy Egan had to compete for an inside forward berth, and Peter Wilson went to manage Dunfermline.

However, McCartney's biggest scoop at this time was the signing of 'L'il Arthur' Milne. Milne came from Angus, and had been impressing English scouts by scoring freely for second leaguers Dundee United. Liverpool took him to Anfield on trial, but because of a mix-up, his name did not appear on the retained list of either club, and in a flash, McCartney had his signature on a Hibs' form. Milne was immensely popular, with his bobbing action as he ran, and he scored a lot of goals, while being equally capable of putting the ball over the bar from underneath it.

So for the first time in many years, Hibs had a team of promise and excitement, even if their inexperience meant that the big wins didn't

Matt Busby introduces the Scotland players to Field Marshal Montgomery

seem to outnumber the big defeats at first. Hibs scored six goals against Clyde in a game which marked the debut of another teenage talent, Bobby Nutley from Blantyre Vics, and five against Arbroath, but lost heavily to Hamilton, Aberdeen and Partick Thistle. By Christmas, the relegation issue seemed to be settled for once without Hibs being involved, and with Kilmarnock and Morton some way adrift.

But Kilmarnock were to bridge the gap, and a spectacular dog-fight ensued drawing in more than half the teams in the league. Hibs were unbeaten from mid-December until they lost to Falkirk at the end of March, but they were still only two points ahead of the three clubs sharing second-bottom spot. Dundee were the unlucky ones who lost out, and so it was an important game in which Hibs beat them in April, because, although Hibs finished in the top half of the league, their thirty-five points were only three more than the Taysiders. There were six sides on thirty-three points. Hibs were the only side to beat Dundee twice, whereas Dundee even beat Rangers by 6–1 in their vain bid for survival.

Wartime

The war seems to have come as a surprise to Scotland's football authorities at least, because their first actions showed little thought or reason. The league kicked off as usual, but was abandoned suddenly after five games when war was actually declared. In the absence of any pattern, odd friendlies were played, before the League decided that without any actual hostilities following the declaration of them the league programme should re-start.

No more games were played before another change in plan, and eastern and western divisions were set up. For the teams in the east, as usual this meant no less travelling but decidedly less gate money. Rangers took the western division, Falkirk the eastern, in quite different fashions—when Falkirk's goals for and against was 42–19, Rangers was 21–2. Cowdenbeath dropped out halfway through, and Arbroath indicated their intent of following suit at the end of the season.

For Hibs the season had seemed likely to continue the improving trend, with a further crop of youngsters coming through— Cuthbertson, Macleod, Ross, Gilmartin and Shaw among them, and even after the war had started, only Ross was an early conscript into the forces. Overall they averaged a point a game to finish eighth of fifteen. Meanwhile the Home Office had set limits on crowds, to limit the risks of bombing raids claiming more lives than was necessary—first five thousand and then eight, and twenty-five thousand were exceptionally allowed at the Hibs-Hearts New Year derby.

Not only was the crowd exceptional, so was the game. Hibs led 3–2 when the half-time whistle sounded. Once in the pavilion, the official realised he had blown too early, and took the teams back out for two minutes. It was not reported how many of the Hibs' players went back out, because Hearts scored twice in these two minutes. Hearts went on to win 6–5, but much of the entertainment was lost on the spectators because of fog. So much so, that at full-time, the teams left the pitch without the Hearts goalkeeper, who did not know the game had ended.

At the end of that first season of confusion, the leading clubs managed themselves into the Southern League, of whose sixteen sides, only Hibs, Hearts and Falkirk came from the Eastern League, and this set-up lasted throughout the remainder of the war; there was no professional football north of the Forth. Hibs had enlisted the services of the Adams and Macleod partnership who had been in East Fife's cupwinning team a few years earlier, but a bigger coup was to induce Bobby Baxter, the Scotland and Middlesbro' centre-half who had been guesting with Hearts, to cross the city. Hibs finished third in the Southern League's inaugural season, and their wins included a 7–1 thrashing of Falkirk, considered by those who knew about these things to be the best of the eastern sides.

Gordon Smith

Baxter's signing was a big feather in manager McCartney's hat, but his major scoop undoubtably turned out to be that of Gordon Smith in April 1941, a story which bears re-telling. Smith had moved from Edinburgh to Montrose at a very early age, and was growing up a Hearts' supporter in Angus. With the introduction of the Southern League, there was no senior football on Tayside, but the juniors continued, and Smith, not yet seventeen, played for Dundee North End and was included in a junior select to play a Hibs-Hearts select. In these days Smith was a centre, and the visiting centre-half was Bobby Baxter. The juniors pulled off a 3–2 win, and Smith scored a hat-trick.

In the following day's papers, the Hearts' chairman was quoted that it had been agreed that Smith was going to Tynecastle, and Smith himself was not sure whether his club had been able to transfer him without his even knowing. Nothing more was heard, until ten days later, when the postponed New Year derby between Hearts and Hibs at Tynecastle was to be played. To everyone's surprise, Hibs fielded three seventeen year-olds, Smith, Bobby Combe and Jock Weir. None was listed in the press. Hibs won 5–3, and Smith scored another hat-trick still at centre, this time against Jimmy Dykes, another international centre-half.

Rumours were rife how this had come about, and the story went that Smith had come down to Edinburgh to play for Hearts, but had been met at the station by McCartney, who persuaded him on the way to the ground that his future lay with Hibs. McCartney's powers of persuasion were certainly formidable, but this explanation exaggerated them a little. The truth was that, instead of announcing his intentions to the world, McCartney had gone unannounced to Montrose. Hearts had offered Smith a trial, but McCartney offered him the £10 signing on fee there and then, and got the signature he wanted.

To rub salt into the wounds, Hearts had also been watching Bobby Combe, as lately as two days before the Tynecastle match, with a view to signing, but McCartney beat them to his signature too. Combe also scored at Tynecastle that night. The following years showed just how much Hearts lost.

Meanwhile, the news for Hibs' fans continued to be better than any of them could remember. Jimmy Caskie, Everton's international winger, came to Easter Road when most expected Falkirk to get his signature, and Matt Busby, from Liverpool, was posted to Kelso and was able to guest for Hibs for more than a year. Hibs' complement of guests also included Alex Hall, a tigerish fullback with the twenty yard tackle considered an indispensible feature of fullback play at the time, from Sunderland, and Bob Hardisty, an amateur wing-half from Wolves, whose inclination to chase the ball wherever it went on the pitch riled his captain, Baxter, on many an occasion. And then there was the Summer Cup!

The 1941 Summer Cup

The Summer Cup had been the inspiration of Harry Swan, who was beginning to believe his ten year forecast for Hibs was closer to the mark than had seemed likely at times. It was run on a knock-out basis, and Hibs beat Celtic, Clyde after a replay, and Dumbarton to reach the final against Rangers. Matt Busby made his debut in the second leg against Clyde.

In the final, Rangers were two goals up in the opening twenty minutes, a position in which they were widely regarded as impregnable, but just on the interval Milne was tripped inside the penalty area, and Finnegan scored from the spot. After an hour, Finnegan equalised. Rangers had a game on their hands now, and with three minutes to go they lost it. In 1941, centre-halves usually had the sole job of marking the opposing centre-forwards rather than going upfield for every set-piece as happens nowadays. Bobby Baxter's trip into the Rangers' penalty area was therefore a rarity, and even more so was the headed goal he scored from Nutley's corner. Hibs won 3–2, and Sammy Kean for one still believes that it was the best Hibs' performance he ever saw.

Pieces of Eight

Given what happened a couple of months later, that was praise indeed. Rangers had already opened up a gap at the top of the league when they visited Easter Road on Spetember 27th, and there was little doubt that they were set on avenging their defeat. The quota crowd was 15,000, but many more were inside the ground, having taken more than usual time to get there because of the problems with a one shilling and one penny admission charge. Those who were late missed Milne's opening goal in seven minutes, but were probably in time for Rangers' equaliser. No-one would have been surprised when Baxter's innocuous tackle on Smith resulted in a penalty, which Venters converted, but things went downhill for the Ibrox men after that, not least for their scorer who was sent off in the second half after a disagreement with Kean. However, Jerry Dawson in goal had a terrific game, which was just as well, as even he lost seven further goals—four to Combe, two to Smith and another to Milne—for Rangers' biggest competitive

The Hibs team of 1943–44

defeat anywhere. Dawson, to his credit, did not lose his sense of humour. Milne would have notched his hat-trick with Hibs' ninth after he had rounded the goalkeeper late on, but, as he had a habit of doing, he missed that easiest of chances. Dawson merely asked him if he had stopped trying.

The return at Ibrox at Yuletide was a frenzied affair, with Rangers throwing everything at a makeshift Hibs' side which had suffered late call-offs from Milne and Baxter, and had Kean as an emergency centre-half. Kean was outstanding, and with Shaw and Hall keeping Rangers' wingers subdued, the first half was goalless without Hibs managing one attack. The second half started in much the same fashion, but this time Hibs did manage a counter attack. Smith led it, and Combe finished it off with the game's only goal. It took the wind completely from Rangers' sails, and Hibs held on for an astonishing result.

These three results against Rangers in about six months gave Hibs the confidence their young side needed, and were undoubtedly the foundation of their continued challenge to Rangers during the rest of the war and beyond. They took twelve league points out of twenty-four against Rangers, and their five wins were also far ahead of anyone else.

Of the four cup finals which Rangers did not win, Hibs won two, and were unlucky in a third.

Another Final

That was the Summer Cup final of 1942, and it was marred by ill-feeling. Milne was seen as the danger-man, and Hibs' performances always seemed to pick up when he was available. Bur Rangers were 'rather ruthless' and Milne was available for only four minutes, after which his colleagues had to soldier on without him. There were no goals, and the nearest was when Davie Shaw struck the woodwork for Hibs. The tie-break in these days was on corners, and these too were level, so that the final was decided on a toss of a coin. Rangers victory was probably one of their hollowest, and they attracted equal press criticism for their celebrations as their means of achieving it.

Hibs were able to compete with Rangers in the one-off situations, but the strength in depth of the Glasgow club told as they won all the wartime league titles. They were well placed—literally—to benefit from the shipyard workers being exempt from being called up, whereas at one time twenty Hibs'players were in the forces from a playing staff which was smaller anyway. However, Robb's shipyard in Leith gave Hibs the regular availability of some top players; they were especially strong at half back, where Matt Busby showed that he was a first class half back behind the teenage partnership of Smith and Finnegan. When Busby moved on after a year or so, Finnegan stepped back when necessary, but Hibs also had Bob Hardisty and Sammy Kean at wing half. Bobby Baxter completed the line until he went back to Hearts in 1945, and the red haired Peter Aird came in. Davie Shaw and Hall were full-back partners, the former moving to the left flank when Jock Goven earned the No. 2 shirt, and Hugh Howie was able to play at full-back or half-back. In goal Jimmy Kerr remained until well after the war, and shared the position during hostilities notably with Joe Crozier of Brentford and Jock Brown of Clyde and Hamilton. Crozier is famous as the first name in the team which beat Rangers 8–1, Brown because his son Gordon is nowadays wheeled on as a TV rugby expert.

In attack, Smith and Caskie were usually available, but the other positions were chopped and changed almost on a weekly basis. Others came back as their duties allowed, Milne, Cuthbertson, Nutley and others and in particular Bobby Combe, who once had to arrange for the press to list him as Hugh Howie because he was on sick leave. An outstanding recruit was Willie Bogan from Renfrew Juniors, who made such an impact that within a couple of years of his debut he was selected to play for Scotland against England. Since Bogan broke his leg in the first minute and was never chosen again, his remains the shortest international career on record.

Back to 1942, and with Cuthbertson home and Milne able to play more than half the games, Hibs were well placed. In addition, Smith had his best season with twenty-six goals and Aberdeen winger Pearson guested on the left, so that Hibs were able to build a substantial lead in the league by Christmas. Unfortunately a few lapses not only cost them the title, but also enabled Morton, another shipbuilding team, to pip them for second place. The big game again was against Rangers, this time the league game at Easter Road in January. There was considerable ill-feeling once more. Venters was involved again, scoring the opening goal and so was Baxter, with Hibs' equaliser from a penalty. Cuthbertson had a goal disallowed four minutes after the break and then Dawson was hurt when he was struck on the head with a missile from the crowd and had to be replaced by Scott Symon. The game drifted from there to a bad-tempered 1–1 draw.

Another Trophy

The next head to head was the 1944 Southern League Cup final. The league cup was run in sections of four teams, with the winners qualifying for the semi-finals. Surprisingly, 1944 was the only year Hibs won their section, on that occasion from Third Lanark, Morton and Albion Rovers, before accounting for Clyde in the semi-finals. The final against Rangers brought back memories of earlier clashes. Again there were no goals, and again the losers played most of the game one player short and again there was scant sympathy on the part of the winners. This time it was Dawson who was hurt in a clash with Bogan. Corners were still the basis of a tie-break, and with three minutes of injury time to go, these were level at five apiece. Then Jimmy Caskie forced another corner on Hibs' left, it was acclaimed as if a goal had been scored and Hibs had another cup.

VE Day

By the autumn of 1944, the Allies were in northern France and thoughts turned to peace. In Edinburgh football, the Allison Cup was introduced in August, eventually to replace the out-dated Rosebery Charity Cup. Aston Villa were the first visitors to take on a Hibs-Hearts select at Tynecastle, and won 4–3. The Rosebery Cup had just one more outing. VE Day was May 8th, and the following evening, a jubilant throng filled Easter Road for the Rosebery final. It could scarcely have been closer, Hibs winning by the odd corner, after a corner flag had stood between Hearts and a last-minute 'equaliser'. To celebrate, the teams were entertained in the boardroom to tea and a selection of solos by Kenny McCrae, the 'well-known Gaelic tenor'. It is nice to record a board pulling out all the stops to please the players.

By August, victory had been assured also in the far east, but too late for football to organise itself for that season. Clubs regrouped as fast as they could, with players coming or going home. Alex Hall went back to Sunderland, Bobby Baxter to Hearts, while Caskie signed for Rangers and Bogan for Celtic, for the large sum of £5,000, which showed the plight of Celtic at the time. Hibs signed Tommy Aitkenhead from Queens Park to replace Caskie.

So the Southern League entered its last season with two divisions and included Aberdeen, the most northerly team to play in the Southern League. Queen of the South were also back after five years, and got off to the best of starts by beating Hibs 3–0. Rangers won the league of course, with Hibs finishing third behind Aberdeen. And by the spring of 1946, the powers that be had made the spontaneous decision to hold a Victory Cup.

Hibs eliminated Dundee with some difficulty in the first round, and then drew Hearts at home in the second. The 40,000 crowd to see Aitkenhead's debut and Tommy Walker's return was a ground record, and they saw Hibs win 3–1. Hibs then beat Partick Thistle and Clyde to reach the final against Rangers, the most appropriate finish to the years of wartime football. Unfortunately this time they were soundly beaten, with the first goal coming from a deflection by Finnegan. Aitkenhead crashed in the equaliser seconds before half-time, but Rangers made the perfect response, with Duncanson scoring seconds into the second half and adding another later for a 3–1 win.

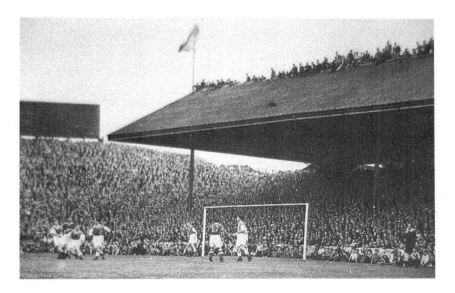

Pittodrie is packed for Hibs' visit in 1947

The Post-war Period

Peacetime football kicked off on August 10th 1946, and it did not take Hibs long to establish their credentials. They started by scoring nine goals against Queen of the South, and four days later they won at Ibrox. Slip-ups at Motherwell, Tynecastle and Aberdeen set them back a little, so that when Rangers visited Easter Road in December, it was vital for Hibs to take both points. Willie Ormond, recently bought from Stenhousemuir, scored his first goal for Hibs, but that was only a late equaliser, and so Hibs failed to narrow the gap. Further points dropped to Morton and Motherwell in January meant that the title was going to Ibrox, but Hibs finished second, five points ahead of Aberdeen.

With only sixteen teams in Division A, the league cup was continued from ite wartime beginnings, and the sections were played in the autumn—Hibs qualified from Third Lanark and Celtic who were bottom of the league—and the knock-out stages were delayed until March. Hibs met Airdrie, and after a 4–4 draw at Broomfield and no goals after two hours at Easter Road, the tie went to sudden death. Witnesses swear that the moon was visible by the time Willie Finnegan settled the issue.

The semi-final was against Rangers and 125,000 people saw Rangers, in determined mood win by three goals to one, and so get their own back for their Scottish Cup defeat a little earlier. That had been at Easter Road, and the fifty thousand spectators was probably a new record for the ground. In a dramatic finish, Smith set up goals for Ormond and Cuthbertson in the last six minutes, for a 2–0 win. Hibs then beat Dumbarton in a low key encounter, to reach the semi-finals.

The Longest Day

In that game, Eddie Turnbull, making one of his first appearances, put Hibs ahead with a penalty, then Kilmarnock equalised. That was strange since Hibs were playing Motherwell, but in fact their full-back was called Kilmarnock. What really took the game into the record books was its length. After extra time, the teams were still locked at 1–1, and a further twenty-two minutes passed before Hugh Howie, one of the least expected to break the deadlock, swung at a ball in midfield and was as surprised as anyone to see the ball sail into the net to do just that. In the other semi-final Aberdeen needed 130 minutes to get past Arbroath.

So the final was against Aberdeen, and although Cuthbertson scored in the opening minute, Aberdeen led 2–1 at the interval. The full-time score was the same, but by then Aberdeen had missed a penalty and were good winners.

By the start of the next season, Hibs seemed to have their strongest team yet; not only had Turnbull put pressure on Combe and Cuthbertson at inside forward, but Hibs had signed Leslie Johnstone from Clyde for a five figure sum. Jock Weir had gone to Blackburn, but Hibs made another major signing in Alex Linwood, Middlesbro's wartime-capped centre. Lawrie Reilly was another coming through, and seemed to be competing with Ormond for the left wing position, so that this level of competition convinced Aitkenhead that a move to Motherwell was in his best interests.

Over three hundred thousand people saw the opening Saturday league cup-ties. Despite being strong favourites, not only did Hibs lose 2–1 to Hearts, but they repeated the feat in the return sectional fixture and the September league derby. They also lost at Ibrox, but Rangers were dropping points too, so that when Hibs beat Partick Thistle in November, it was the Firhill side that they replaced at the top. Smith in paricular was in top form during the autumn, with a truly memorable goal—awesome would be the modern word—at Motherwell, five goals against Third Lanark and a superb last-minute winner against Dundee.

So Hibs were top of the league at New Year, and a derby win against Hearts who were bottom strengthened their position. Rangers however had games in hand, and the meeting of the two at Easter Road on the last day of January was keenly anticipated.

Before that however, Hibs had to travel to Coatbridge to meet Albion Rovers in the cup. They won win 2–0, Cuthbertson scoring twice, but what neither the players or the crowd was aware of was that in the stand, manager McCartney had collapsed, and he died later the same day. His legacy to Hibs was the most talented team in the country, poised in the short term for their first championship in forty-five years, and beyond that to be the best team in Europe.

— 7 —

THE FAMOUS FIVE

Hugh Shaw, who had been trainer for the previous ten years or so was immediately appointed manager, with his contemporary Jimmy McColl stepping up from assistant trainer to take over Shaw's job.

The new manager's first selection was of the team to meet Rangers. It was an emotional occasion, and a game in the best tradition between the sides. The much vaunted 'iron curtain' seemed impregnable until the last minute when the Rangers' defenders along with just about everybody else thought that there was no chance of Linwood reaching a long ball heading out of play, but they were all wrong, and Cuthbertson had a free header from the cross to give Hibs two valuable points.

Even so, Rangers' games in hand looked sufficient for the Ibrox side to take the title. Hibs were in top form, scoring four goals away to St Mirren and Celtic, but they needed the unexpected bonus of Queens Park's winning at Ibrox. In Hibs' second last game they scored five times against Motherwell, and at that point needed just a point in their last game, away to Dundee. In the meantime, Rangers dropped another point at Motherwell and so could not catch Hibs, which was just as well since the Easter Road side lost 3–1 at Dens Park.

Rangers did get some measure of revenge in the cup, in a semi-final played before a crowd of 143,570. This stands as a British record for a club game other than a final, and is likely to stay that way. The game swung on a single error by George Farm deputising for Kerr, when he missed a cross to give Rutherford the easiest of scores. It is a surprising fact that Farm played only nine first team games for Hibs, before moving to Blackpool, (and a cup winners' medal in the 'Matthews final').

There was quick recognition of Hibs' new status as no fewer than five Hibs men were included in the Scotland team that beat Belgium

Gordon Smith—an artist's impression of an artist. (courtesy of HFC Museum)

2–0, and the strength of the pool was evident in Hibs' tour of Belgium, when, minus all five, they started with only an odd goal defeat from Standard Liege.

For a team with Hibs' new aspirations, season 1948–49 was a disappointment. Far too many points went adrift, none more unexpected than the one that Albion Rovers grabbed at Easter Road after trailing 4–1 with ten minutes to go. Hibs did top the league in November, but only because Rangers, and Dundee this time, had games in hand, and this time they were to prove vital. Rangers took the title, with the Dens Parkers five points above Hibs.

Hibs also failed to qualify in the league cup, in a strange section in which Rangers won after having only two points at half-way, and

Clyde beat Celtic 6–3. An undistinguished Scottish Cup run, with games against Forfar, Raith and East Fife continued the trend. For good measure, they also lost the McCartney Memorial Match by the only goal to Manchester United.

With Willie Ormond having broken his leg in the spring in a cup-tie against Aberdeen, Lawrie Reilly came in on the left wing, to such effect that he was picked for the Scotland side to play Wales in Cardiff in that role. His potential as a centre had still not been recognised, because even when Linwood was transferred to Clyde in December, Angus Plumb and Cuthbertson were each given the chance to establish himself, and it was only in the spring, when Ormond was back to full form that Reilly was given the no. 9 shirt.

That meant that four fifths of Scotland's most famous quintet were in place. Bobby Combe and Cuthbertson were competing for the inside right position, but the youthful Bobby Johnstone was getting rave notices in the reserves, and was given a chance in the first team for the friendly with Nithsdale Wanderers at Sanquhar on April 21st. That was therefore the first public appearance of the five, and their second was in a charity match in Belfast.

But for the opening of the new season in August 1949, it was as before, with Combe the man in possession. The big change came only in October. Hibs had lost to Dunfermline Athletic in the league cup semi-final at Tynecastle, and the half-backs got most of the blame. The entire line of Gallagher, McNeil and Cairns was dropped for Combe, Paterson and Buchanan. Archie Buchanan was another wing-half who had started as an inside forward. Cuthbertson and Plumb had by this time moved on, so the way was open for Johnstone to step in. The new forward line made its collective league debut on October 15th against Queen of the South, and Hibs won 2–0. The half-back line proved such a success that they stayed together for several years, and initially all the talk was about them. It was only later that the forwards' exploits started to eclipse them.

Meanwhile, Gordon Smith had taken over from Davie Shaw as captain. With 29 goals, was Hibs' top scorer for the seventh year out of eight, a remarkable tally for a winger, and led his men to their best season so far. Apart from their league cup exit at Tynecastle, Hibs lost at the same ground in the September derby, but thereafter dropped only one more point to New Year, because of Celtic's last-minute equaliser at Parkhead. Hearts 'Terrible Trio' were also on the go by now, in fact they came together before Hibs' five were complete, and by New Year they had strung together twelve straight league wins, so that excitement about the clash on January 2nd was intense.

Edinburgh's largest football crowd ever turned up, 65,850 in number, or about the capacity of the newly completed Murrayfield, and there were many complaints from those who saw little for their money. Those who were better placed saw a vintage Hibs' performance in the first half capped by a splendid headed goal by Smith, and a first-class second-half showing from the Tynecastle men with goals from Conn and Wardhaugh to take the points.

Hibs were quickly back into their stride, however, and lost just one more league game. Co-incidentally it marked the only first team appearance at Easter Road of Lew Goram, father of Andy, but unfortunately he was on loan to Third Lanark and had a shut-out. Thirds won by the only goal. The game at Easter Road against Celtic was remarkable for Eddie Turnbull's hat-trick of penalties, and Celtic's goal in a 4–1 defeat also came from the spot.

Hearts had not been able to maintain their form, and the league developed into a two-horse race, Hibs and Rangers. Another crowd

Tommy Younger punches clear in a match against Aberdeen

in excess of a hundred thousand turned out for Hibs last game that they had to win. But this time they failed to breach the home defence, and a goalless draw resulted. Nowadays, Rangers' performance would have been extolled, but in 1950 crowds did not like or expect teams to try harder to prevent goals than score them, and there was a less than celebratory atmosphere. Rangers still had to take a point from Third Lanark in their outstanding fixture, and this they did, after Thirds missed a late penalty with the score at 2–2.

Hibs therefore finished second, with forty-nine points. That was more than they got from the same number of games in each of their title-winning seasons, and they scored twenty goals more than the champions.

By the start of the new season, the confidence which exuded from Easter Road that at last Hibs were poised to topple Rangers did not seem misplaced. They had the necessary reserve strength, often a weakness in comparison with the Ibrox side, and indeed the Hibs' reserves were going through an eight year spell where they were only losing about twice a year. Hibs had also completed a successful summer tour, beating Tottenham Hotspur en route to the continent, where they beat Bayern München 6–1 as well as Augsburg, the best team in central Europe, by 4–2.

They started off at whirlwind pace, winning all five sectional league cup ties—the last one at Dundee was abandoned in a storm and not replayed because Hibs could not be caught, but they found the rest of the tournament harder. Firstly they had to overcome Aberdeen in the quarter-finals, a feat made more difficult by the 4–1 reverse in the first leg at Pittodrie. Gordon Smith missed that game through injury, but he and manager Shaw hatched a plan for the return four days later. Smith was not named in the team, and when he appeared in the Hibs' dressing room shortly before kick-off, the players expected him to wish them well. Instead Smith stripped and put on the No. 7 shirt, about the same time as a huge roar announced the crowd's reaction to his being in the side. Even the winger later admitted that the expression on Aberdeen, and of course ex-Hibs, captain Davie Shaw's face at the toss-up told Smith that his very presence was worth a goal of a start.

And within three minutes, centre-half Young had scored a panicky own goal, and the chase was on. With the early kick-off, the ground was only half full at kick-off, but by half-time, there were sixty thousand there. There had still only been one goal, but Johnstone and Ormond scored within a five minute spell, and the game went to extra-time. Reilly scored within a minute of the start of the extra period, but a famous victory was denied when a late and speculative effort by Yorston ended up in Younger's net. It took two further games to settle the issue, both in Glasgow, Hibs winning 5–1 after a one each draw.

A semi-final against Queen of the South at Tynecastle was a benign draw, and a Turnbull hat-trick sealed that one after Queens had taken the lead, and it left Hibs to take on Motherwell in the final, a side they had beaten 6–2 on their own ground a week before. The final could not have been more different.

It was never quite clear why on some occasions, given their reserve strength, manager Shaw played the one-footed Willie Ormond at inside left when Turnbull was unavailable, but this was a case in point. Although Hibs attacked for an hour, the attack looked lop-sided, and they failed to make the breakthrough. Then Motherwell scored twice in three minutes in classic fashion and one of Hibs' best chances to win a national cup had gone. Just before the end, Younger kicked the ground and the ball trundled to Watters who lobbed the Hibs' keeper to complete the disaster.

The league of course was the main target, but Hibs had lost two of their three first games to Aberdeen and Hearts. Following that, though, they only dropped one further point before New Year, to a bizarre own goal by centre-half Paterson, who put the ball over Younger's head from halfway at Ibrox. By now they were third, but with games ahead over Dundee and Aberdeen, and, despite losing again to Hearts, did their chances no harm by demolishing the Dons 6–2 on January 2nd.

They only lost one more league game on the run-in, by a single goal at Airdrie, and the title was wrapped up when a side packed with reserves beat Clyde 4–0 at Shawfield. By the time Hibs met the Old Firm over the last week-end, they were home by a street. Rangers were outclassed in a way seldom seen as Hibs led 4–0 before a last minute consolation score for the losers. Hibs beat Celtic 3–1 on the Monday, and after a thirty game programme, they finished with a ten point lead over Rangers.

Hibs also had the ascendancy over their Ibrox rivals in a titanic struggle in a first round Scottish Cup match at Ibrox in front of another six figure crowd. They looked a little unsure after Simpson had given Rangers the lead in the opening moments, but had fought back to deserve the equaliser they got when Smith volleyed home from the penalty spot. Just after half-time, Simpson scored again, and Hibs had it all to again. Few sides came back once at Ibrox, never mind twice in these days, but Turnbull got Hibs' second equaliser with one of the cannonball efforts which were his speciality. Then, with nine minutes going, the light blue wall faced up to another free kick, but this time a quick passing movement from Turnbull to Ormond to Johnstone ended with the little inside man sending the ball high into Rangers' net.

A hat-trick by Reilly at Broomfield saw Hibs into the semi-finals, against Motherwell at Tynecastle, and, far from avenging their Hampden defeat, came off even worse. They were a goal down before left-back Ogilvie broke his leg after quarter of an hour, causing some reorganisation, and the inside forwards drawn deeper. Later on

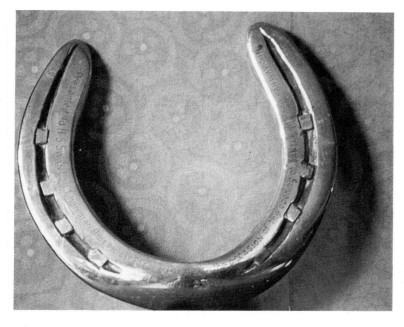

Horse shoe presented to Harry Swan at the opening of the Easter Road railway halt. (courtesy of HFC Museum)

Ormond ruptured ligaments, the worst of many serious injuries he suffered, and too much sting had been drawn from the Hibs' attack. They fought well and Reilly scored two good goals, but had to concede defeat by 3–2.

It was a busy summer, with a tour to France, the Festival of Britain and the St Mungo's Cup, a knock-out tournament for Division A sides before the domestic season kicked off again. Hibs had played under floodlights in Paris for the first time, an idea which took a trick with the forward looking Mr. Swan, and led to Hibs playing the first floodlit game in Scotland, at Ochilview against Stenhousemuir, before having their own lights installed in 1954.

The Hibs' chairman was very progressive in many ways, such as the floodlights and playing foreign sides, but he also had some ideas which would have been less fruitful. One was a plan to increase the capacity of Easter Road to 98,000, by increasing the terracing all round the ground. In fact, only the section opposite the stand was heightened in the fifties, and even that was not needed very often as the numbers attending football began a steady fall. Also, there was no thought of covering or seating any part of the ground other than the main stand, and little improvement was evident in other facilities for food, toilets etc.

There was no move either to replace the stand, which had by then reached the end of its expected life, so that of the vast gate receipts which the huge attendances of the times generated, there was little to be seen in the way of investment—Hibs did not even have to buy players, and those they had were subject to the maximum wage in force at the time. Some improvements were made, notably the railway halt near the Bothwell Street bridge, which brought football special trains virtually to the gates of Easter Road, and the terracing was gradually concreted during the second part of the fifties, but even the railway stop showed that Swan did not foresee the change towards motor transport which had soon started.

Anyway, back in 1951, hopes were high, but it was a disappointing season, despite, strange to say, Hibs retaining their league title. They failed to qualify from a league cup section which included Partick Thistle, Motherwell and Stirling Albion, and lost their first Scottish Cup tie at Kirkcaldy. Their league form was better, with no losses in the first nine games, a win against early leaders East Fife, and a draw with Rangers, and by the end of the year they were top. This was partly because Rangers, who had qualified in the league cup, had games in hand, and the question as often was whether these games would be enough. Hibs drew an important game at Ibrox, which seemed to shade the balance in their favour, then undid that good work by losing 5–2 to Queen of the South.

At that stage, Hibs were three points ahead, with two home games left, against Rangers' four away ones. The problem was that there were still two months of the season to run, and so by the time that Hibs beat Dundee 2–1, it was enough to take the title. While Rangers had been dropping the odd point to give Hibs their chance, Hibs had had to play out time with a series of friendlies, mostly in England. Only one Saturday league game in the last eight weeks of the season an unsatisfactory way to end it.

Five Hundred Up

Gordon Smith had become the third player to score a hundred competitive goals for Hibs during the season, wartime games excluded, and he reached another landmark with his five hundredth appearance for the club in the opening league cup-tie against Queen of the South. It was not a vintage display by any means, or even a win, but Hibs did qualify from the group, and the quarter finals against Morton brought a goal avalanche. Hibs scored six goals in the Saturday game at Greenock and a further six against Morton on the following Wednesday at Easter Road, and finished off the week by beating Hearts 3–1.

On the Monday between the two league cup ties, English champions Manchester United came north for Smith's testimonial game. On an unforgettable evening, the Mancunians led 3–2 at the interval despite having a goal disallowed; in the second half the tables were turned with a vengeance, and Hibs won 7–3—despite having a goal disallowed. Turnbull, with four goals including a penalty, Reilly, Smith and Ormond were the Hibs scorers.

The number seven kept cropping up. On five separate occasions, Hibs hit seven goals in the league; Motherwell were worst hit, losing that number twice, and seven to Reilly alone. The magic number also featured at Highbury, in Hibs first appearance before TV cameras, and

Jock Govan in determined mood against Dunfermline Athletic at Tynecastle

(presumably) their first before HRH the Duke of Edinburgh. They lost 7–1.

Statistically it was a curious season, a three horse race with the other thirteen teams on less than a point a game. East Fife fell out of contention late on, but finished nine points ahead of Hearts who were fourth. By the middle of February, Hibs led Rangers by three points with two fewer games to go. They only lost once more, but nevertheless lost the title on goal average. Had goal difference been introduced, they would have won it.

In an entertaining summer, Hibs beat Tottenham Hotspur and Newcastle United to reach the Coronation Cup final against Celtic— Celtic won 2–0—and, at a time when many sides had yet to cross the channel, they took on a three game trip to Brazil. With no concessions to the climate in clothing or style of play, they lost twice and drew with Vasco da Gama.

There is little doubt that by 1953–54, this great side had peaked. For the early part of that season, Reilly was in dispute over a benefit, but re-signed at the end of September. Bobby Combe was captain now; the rumbustious Willie McFarlane took over from Govan at right-back, and Pat Ward came in as Hugh Howie's health failed. Howie had one outstanding memory to legate; Hibs had reached the league cup semi-finals, and played East Fife at Tynecastle. The Fifers were 1–0 up with ten minute remaining; Reilly scored twice in a minute to put Hibs in front, but twice Howie handled blatantly to give the fearsome penalty taker Emery the chances to give East Fife a 3–2 win.

That apart, things went pretty well until December 5th, when Smith broke a leg, and Buchanan suffered severe ligament damage. Reilly then contracted pleurisy, which kept him out of the 1954 World Cup in Switzerland. Hibs finished fifth. Rangers post-war team were also past their best and were fourth, behind winners Celtic and, of all people, Hearts and Partick Thistle.

It was in October 1954 that things became brighter at Easter Road. The new floodlighting, or 'drenchlighting' system was opened with a game against Hearts which the visitors won by 2–0. Reilly was still not back, but Tommy Preston had been a more than able deputy, with eight goals in the league cup qualifying matches. By now Turnbull was captain, and other new faces coming into the first XI were John Grant, Jimmy Thomson, and Jackie Plenderleith, as the side faced a period of major transition.

Laurie Reilly heads for goal against Airdrie

It was not helped by Hearts scoring five against them in the New Year derby, and again at the end of the month in a cup-tie, or that Bobby Johnstone was transferred to Manchester City about the same time for £22,000. Even Hibs' supporters can be fickle on occasion, and fewer than a thousand packed the enormous stadium to watch the end of season tussle with Stirling Albion. On a brighter note, Gordon Smith was picked to captain Scotland on their European tour, where they recorded their first ever win against Austria. Scotland's form seemed to have declined with Hibs and Rangers, and they had just lost 7–2 at Wembley. When Smith returned he resumed the captaincy of Hibs.

There were two new competitions to take part in in 1955–56, and there were those who thought that Hibs were playing too many games. There was the European Cup, organised by the French sportspaper L'Equipe on an invitational basis, and there was also the Anglo-Scottish Floodlit League.

Hibs were invited by L'Equipe because of their involvement and popularity on the continent, rather than that they had won most points since 1946. Their first opponents were Rotweiß Essen, the champions of the World Cupwinners West Germany. The Scottish press was less than impressed, and in fact not represented in the Ruhrgebiet, where Hibs delighted thousands of UK servicemen by demolishing their hosts 4–0 in a mudbath. It was just as well, as Smith, Reilly and Younger could not get back from a trip to Denmark in time for the second leg, which finished 1–1.

The second round brought Djurgaarden from Stockholm to Scotland. Because of a winter closedown in Scandinavia, both games were here, Hibs winning the away leg 3–1 at Firhill, and the home one by the only goal. This took them to the semi-finals, where they met Stade Reim from France. The first game was in Paris, and Hibs seemed to have done well to lose only one goal until in the final minute they lost another. The second leg was the first of their great European nights down the Easter Road slope, but attack as the might, fortune and a breakthrough eluded them, and in a classic breakaway, Glovakic scored the only goal for the visitors.

The Anglo-Scottish Cup was a more sedate affair. The Scottish clubs played only the English clubs so there might have been some difficulty in determining a winner. That there was not was largely

Left. The great Gordon Smith
Right. Bobby Combe with Jock Stein of Celtic

because many fixtures were not fulfilled. The odd thing was that Hearts were included—they did not have floodlights.

In the domestic season, Hibs failed to qualify in the league cup, finished a reasonable fourth in the league, and, along with Hearts, made history in the cup. Hibs' contribution was to play in the first floodlit tie, against Raith Rovers. Hearts' is recorded elsewhere.

If there were any lingering doubts about the shift of the balance of football power in the capital, they were all resolved in the opening league cup-tie of 1956–57. Eddie Turnbull scored a good goal in the early minutes, but Hearts then scored five. It was a new and very youthful Hibs' defence now, especially with Jackie Wren coming straight in to replace Tommy Younger who had gone to Liverpool.

The one outstanding performance of that season was Hibs' only Scottish Cup game, at home to Aberdeen. The first twenty-eight minutes were a nightmare, with the Hibs' defence torn asunder by the running of Leggat, Buckley and Hather, and Aberdeen led by four goals at that point. Yet Hibs almost turned it round after the interval.

The Rangers defence is dejected—Bobby Johnstone has just put Hibs 3–2 up in the 1951 Scottish Cup tie at Ibrox

Bobby Johnstone on target against St Mirren

In two minutes, Smith got one back, and after twenty-five minutes, Reilly swerved in a ball from the byeline for 4–2. Four minutes later, Bobby Nicol rattled in another through a ruck of players, but in a frantic finish, the nearest Hibs came was when Ormond struck the crossbar in the final minute. The crowd was a feature—twenty-seven thousand on a day when a sell-out crowd of 49,000 watched Hearts go down 4–0 to Rangers, and even more saw Scotland beat Wales at Murrayfield. Police cover never seemed to be a problem in these days. Towards the end of the season, Lawrie Reilly was back in the Scotland team—he played in a record fifth appearance against England at Wembley, and his tally of five goals there has likewise yet to be beaten.

Despite the youthfulness of the team, the first half of season 1957–58 went pretty well, and Hibs finished the year second to Hearts, and only a couple of points adrift. This was the season in which Hearts waltzed through their league card with only a single defeat at Shawfield, but Hibs had already two creditable performances against them. They had lost two goals in the opening twelve minutes at Tynecastle in the league, three in twenty-five, at a time when Hearts were scoring eights and nines, but refused to capitulate, and brought it back to 3–1. Then in October, they won 4–2 in a match to hansel the new Tynecastle floodlights. (The floodlit league had finished by now).

It was not Hearts who contributed to Hibs' fall from grace in the second half of the season as much as the tough-tackling Clyde on the last Saturday of 1957. Virtually every one of the Hibs' players who played at Easter Road or in the reserve fixture at Shawfield required treatment after that encounter. The young Joe Baker, the even less experienced Johnny Macleod and Jimmy Harrower were all injured, while at Shawfield, the promising inside forward Alex Marshall had his career effectively ended with a horrific double compound fracture of the leg.

Hibs had a difficult job to raise a recognisable team for the Ne'erday derby, and a 2–0 defeat was acceptable in the circumstances, but their interest in the league had gone—Hearts had it under wraps anyway. Hibs did manage to produce some sterling performances in the cup. After a low-key defeat of second division Dundee United, they were drawn at Tynecastle.

Notwithstanding their earlier victory there, few people gave Hibs

The Joe Baker handball incident in the 1958 Cup final

a chance against the aggressive Gorgie side. Hibs countered their wing-halves Cumming and Mackay by playing John Grant at inside forward. Every Hib played out of his skin that afternoon, but the outcome turned on the performances of two in particular. In goal, the brave Lawrie Leslie was outstanding, and indeed was effectively voted man of the match by many of the more serious newspapers, despite the fact that up front Joe Baker scored four goals in that famous 4–3 triumph. (The author was not allowed to go because there would be too many people there.) It should be noted also that in the (one) season when Hearts seemed invincible, Hibs twice won by scoring four goals at Tynecastle.

Next, Third Lanark came to Easter Road, and a further two goals by Baker saw them off by three goals to two, and Hibs' prize was a semi-final against Rangers at Hampden. It went to two games. The first was drawn 2–2, but the drama came in the second. Hibs led by two goals to one with the final whistle in sight (earshot?). Rangers launched a final assault, Ralph Brand jumped with Leslie, and the ball landed in Hibs' net. Extra time or what? Then, referee Bobby Davidson noticed the bravely raised flag of his linesman, and after a consultation awarded Hibs a free kick for hands. Subsequent photographic evidence

Loving Cup presented by Hearts at opening of Tynecastle floodlights in 1957. (courtesy of HFC Museum)

showed that the linesman had been correct in spotting Brand's offence, and Hibs went through.

Since they had beaten Hearts and Rangers to get there, it was unfortunate that Hibs' opponents in the final were also difficult opponents in Clyde. After the previous encounter the final was little different to the league encounter. Within a quarter of an hour, the threat of Andy Aitken's speed had been neutralised to the point where he could hardly walk. After half an hour, John Baxter had the misfortune to deflect Coyle's shot past Leslie for what turned out to be the only goal. The nearest Hibs came in reply was a 'goal' by Baker in which he used his hand. Turnbull and Ormond, veterans of the 1947 final, worked like Trojans for their last chance of a medal, but to no avail. Smith was absent with an ankle injury and Reilly had retired five days earlier in an emotional farewell in which he had scored against Rangers in a 3–1 win at Easter Road. There was much ill-feeling about losing to these particular opponents in such a manner.

— 8 —
EVENINGS IN EUROPE

When Harry Swan had had the floodlights put in at Easter Road, he foresaw Hibs playing top English teams on a regular basis. Foreign visitors were still something of a novelty, although Rapid Vienna and Bayern München were among those who had come, and Hibs' meetings with continental opposition was usually on close season tours. This was still the case in the late fifties—Hibs played in a tournament in Holland in 1958, toured in Spain a year later and visited Germany and Yugoslavia in 1960. During the sixties and early seventies, it was more commonly the visits of top European sides, that provided the big midweek nights at Easter Road.

These games were mostly in the Fairs Cup, a competition ostensibly for cities which had trade fairs, and Hibs traded loosely on the Edinburgh Festival. A Hibs-Hearts select had accepted an invitation to take part in the second such competition in 1958, but had withdrawn because of Hearts' short-lived involvement in the European Cup. The Fairs Cup took two years to grind to a conclusion—the first one had taken three!—and so Hibs had to wait until 1960 for another chance.

Until then Hibs had enough on their plate to re-create a team with any pretensions of honours. Suddenly the good days seemed far away. Hibs failed to qualify from Aberdeen, Falkirk and Kilmarnock in the league cup, and had four goal defeats from Aberdeen, Hearts and Rangers in the opening third of the league campaign.

The defence was still being marshalled superbly by Eddie Turnbull at wing-half, and provided a blend of youth and experience, but the attack combined youth and enthusiasm of Baker, Macleod, Frye, Aitken and others. They had the perfect fillip when Gordon Smith came back from injury, and lost only three of their next nineteen matches in a run which even included a very welcome win at

Left. Alex Edwards teases the Rangers' defence
Right. Joe Baker shoots for goal against Raith Rovers

Tynecastle. Joe Baker in particular benefitted, with eighteen goals in nine games, including a hat-trick which beat Celtic 3–2. Baker was maturing very quickly as a centre, and the experience of playing with Smith was complemented by that of playing between Bobby Charlton and Jimmy Greaves in England's Under-23 team.

Baker's season, and Hibs', effectively ended in a cup replay against Raith Rovers, at Easter Road, in which he was carried off the field after an incident with Kirkcaldy centre-half McNaught which caused a certain amount of bad feeling. Hibs won 2–1, and Baker missed the next two rounds before returning against Third Lanark at Cathkin in the quarter-finals. It was soon clear that he was less than fit, and he had to swap places with Smith. Then Smith was hurt, and was not to play for Hibs again. Turnbull was also in the wars, and minus all three, Hibs failed to beat Third Lanark, or anyone else for the rest of the season.

Turnbull was not to play again for Hibs either, because by the new season he had become club trainer. Smith was given a free transfer rather than the club incur the cost of a further operation, so the winger paid his own hospital bill and was back for the new season in the maroon of Hearts. He continued for another five years, for Hearts and Dundee, and won championship medals, and played in the European Cup, with both.

Jim Scott, the younger brother of the Rangers' internationalist Alex, and Bobby Nicol took on the heavy responsibility of replacing Smith and Turnbull, while in goal Willie Wilson from Musselburgh took over from Leslie who had gone to Airdrie. John Grant was the new captain and faced a difficult start. In a league cup section Hibs lost all six games and they conceded eleven goals in two games with Rangers, and a two and a half minute hat-trick to Ian St John of Motherwell. To try to bring about the transformation that Smith's return had caused the previous year, Hibs this time brought Bobby Johnstone back from Manchester City. Johnstone made his debut against Kilmarnock, and it was clear that he had lost a smaller proportion of his skill than he had gained in weight since his departure south.

The magic did not work, however, and it was in some desperation

John Blackley explains his actions to the referee

that manager Shaw reverted to Preston and Ormond. This proved to be the catalyst, and initiated a goal blitz. Hibs beat Dunfermline 7–4, and a week later rewrote the record books with an incredible 11–1 win at Airdrie. Baker had hat-tricks in both, and Preston scored four at Airdrie. It was the highest away score in either the Scottish or English leagues, and only the third occasion a visiting side had scored ten—and Hibs did that again eight weeks later by winning 10–2 at Firhill. Almost incidentally they had beaten Bolton 5–2 in midweek, to make it twenty-three goals in a week, and in another midweek frolic they drew 6–6 with Middlesbro'.

That game illustrated that while Hibs games were all very exciting, and Baker's form raised the question of how he would have fared with Smith, Johnstone, Turnbull and Ormond beside him all at once, it also suggested that the defence was less than watertight. So did a 6–4 defeat at Pittodrie and a 5–1 one by Hearts either side of New Year. Hibs finished eighth in the league, scoring a club record of 106 league goals and losing 85; the former was a higher rate per game than the famous five had achieved in any season. Joe Baker notched forty-two of them, to beat Lawrie Reilly's club record by twelve.

It was all exciting stuff, but Hibs were back where they had been a year earlier—Johnstone had been shipped back to Oldham after a disagreement at the club, and so there was a vacancy for an experienced playmaker. Jackie Plenderleith had made an impact at centre-half, and so his move to Manchester City did not help. The result was that Hibs lost their first eight league games. Johnstone was replaced by Sammy Baird, from Rangers, at a considerable cost, and he made his debut at Perth, the same day as Ronnie Simpson, who had come from Newcastle United, in goal and the teenage prodigy Eric Stevenson on the left wing. Hibs lost by 2–0, but the losing sequence was ended with a hat-trick by another newcomer, Bobby Kinloch, in a 4–3 win against St. Mirren. Hibs gradually moved up the table to a safe position, but not in such style to give any indication that their greatest ever result was just around the corner.

Barcelona

Hibs' first Fairs Cup tie was supposed to be against Lausanne Sports, but the Swiss withdrew on the grounds that they did not have a good

Joe Baker's triumphant return to Hibs in 1970—his winner against Aberdeen

enough team. A year later they beat Hearts. The second round paired Hibs with Barcelona, the top side in Europe. Real Madrid got most of the plaudits outside Iberia at the time, and nowhere more than in Scotland where earlier the same year they had scored seven in the European Cup final against Eintracht Frankfurt, who in turn had scored twelve against Rangers in the semi-finals. Real were not Spanish champions, though, as Barcelone had won the local league for the last two seasons. In the current season, Barcelona had ended the interest of their Castillian rivals for the first time, winning 3–1 in Barcelona and Madrid to become undisputed top dogs in Europe when they met Hibs.

That was not as early as was intended, however, as fog ruled out the first leg at Easter Road in November, and so Hibs travelled to the Catalan capital at Christmas time and received scant praise for a fantastic 4–4 draw. They actually led by two goals with six minutes remaining.

The return was in February, and over fifty-three thousand spectators ensured a floodlit ground record for Edinburgh. Baker rose to head home a Macleod cross in ten minutes, and the crowd found room to dance, but the Spaniards dominated most of the period to the interval, and deserved to lead by 2–1 at that point.

They didn't after fifteen minutes of the second half, as Hibs furious assault down the slope showed no signs of flagging and threatened to become irrestible. Another fifteen minutes passed, however, with no breakthrough but increasingly desperate defensive measures on the part of the visitors, at which point Preston headed in from close range following a corner, and there was pandemonium. Hibs launched attack after attack, and might have had a handful of penalties before the one they did get with five minutes to go when Macleod was scythed down. The Spaniards completely lost the place.

For several minutes, the kick could not be taken because of their aggressive behaviour to the referee, and the situation was that even Sammy Baird's nerve—and few thought he had any—betrayed him. Bobby Kinloch, sitting close by on the turf watching the shenanigans, sensed his one chance of footballing immortality, and drove the ball past Medrano into the net. A further riot took place, with the referee this time needing assistance from the police, and the remaining minutes were played out in an unreal atmosphere, until the final whistle confirmed one of European football's biggest upsets.

Roma

Hibs reward for beating Barcelona was a trip to the eternal city, but first the eternal city had to come to them, and an unpleasant first leg finished two apiece. The second leg was only a week later, and manager Shaw confused the Italians by switching the jerseys of Baker and Kinloch. The Italians could not have had very long memories, but the ruse worked, and Kinloch took the bruises as Hibs raced to a 3–1 lead, before Roma scored twice so that a third game was needed. Roma had not only home advantage, but also managed to arrange to be unavailable until a month after the Scottish season had ended, so that they had little difficulty in beating a less than match-fit Hibs' team by six goals to nil. By the time another new season came around, Joe Baker was back in Italy, with Torino, and Johnny Macleod at Arsenal.

Despite the overflowing coffers, the only player brought in was Ally Macleod, a winger with an eccentrically entertaining style from Blackburn Rovers and harbouring no thoughts at that time of

'Romulus and Remus' presented by A.S. Roma, Fairs Cup semi-final, 1961 (courtesy HFC Museum)

Argentina. This was partly because Hibs still had a regular flow of good youngsters coming through—Jim Easton at centre-half and inside forward Davie Gibson were the pick of the current crop—but none of them proved a suitable replacement for Baker, and Hugh Shaw resigned as manager in the autumn. This clearly spurred the chairman to do something about the situation, and before another manager was appointed, Joe's brother Gerry was brought to Scotland. Gerry was perhaps more skilful than Joe, but less aggressive, but his introduction soon took Hibs to a safe position in the league.

Walter Galbraith

Hibs were rebuffed in their efforts to attract Bobby Brown of St Johnstone and Jock Stein of Dunfermline, and so they gave the job to Walter Galbraith, the man who brought Harvey McCreadie to Easter Road. Most Hibs' fans had never heard of him, or knew that he had just taken Tranmere Rovers down into England's Fourth Division. He was apparently a keen student of continental methods. Apart from McCreadie, Galbraith signed Johnny Byrne, Morris Stevenson, Doug

Logan and John Blair. Ally McLeod was Hibs' new skipper for season 1962–63 and the new manager hoped to be among the challengers.

From the start they were nowhere close. An early spate of injuries was blamed, but a run of only one point from the last eight games of 1962 left Hibs one place from the bottom and in serious trouble. At this point the weather took over, and there was no more football until March. This meant playing up to four league games in eight days. Ally McLeod resigned as captain and stop-gap signing Tommy Leishman took over. At one time Hibs were nine points behind Clyde who were third bottom. When they lost at home to Airdrie, it was with the prospect of visiting Parkhead, Ibrox, Dens Park and Firhill within the following week. Hibs took no points home or away from Airdrie, Clyde or Falkirk. Hearts tried to lend Hibs players but were not allowed to. Latterly Hibs ran out of centre-halves—they had used about nine—and were given permission to sign Willie Toner from Kilmarnock.

When Hibs had three games to go, Clyde had two, four points more and a better goal average. Hibs had not strung three wins together all season, so now was a good time to start. Hibs beat St Mirren, and then won 4–0 away to Queen of the South in a match which asked a lot of questions about the Queens' commitment. Clyde lost to Celtic. Hibs last game was away to Raith, already relegated, and the travelling supporters invaded the pitch when Baxter scored the first goal. Hibs went on to win 4–0, leaving Clyde the impossible task of winning by about eight goals—against Rangers.

It was ironic that it was in 1963, when Hibs' fortunes had taken such a dive almost back to the levels of the 1930s, that Harry Swan, who had been instrumental to so much success in between times, should retire as chairman. He was succeeded by his friend, Bill Harrower, a local bookmaker and former pools worker, who was from Gorgie but had season tickets for both Easter Road and Tynecastle. Money was now available, and by the the league cup games, Neil Martin had been signed from Queen of the South, to be followed at intervals by Pat Quinn, from Blackpool, John Parke, the Linfield left-back and Willie Hamilton, the brilliant and tragic inside forward from Hearts.

It was unfortunate that Galbraith did not manage to blend the skills of Hamilton and Quinn into the same side. With serious injuries to

Jock Stein arrives to be Hibs Manager

Easton and Parke, it took some time to form a satisfactory blend, but by mid-season, more youngsters like Billy Simpson, Pat Stanton and Bobby Duncan were showing up well. Hibs were now in a safe position, and manager Galbraith resigned. The conclusion must be that Hibs would probably not have got into that state if money had been available from the Baker and Macleod transfers when it was needed, i.e. immediately, and that Galbraith gave their heads to a number of very good young players.

Jock Stein

The timing of Galbraith's resigning and the fact that Jock Stein had announced he was leaving Dunfermline at the end of the season anyway and then the speed with which he eased himself into the Hibs' job suggested that wheels had been turning for some time.

Stein had an immediate opportunity to assess his new charges. The powers that be had decided that a thirty-four league programme together with a sectional league cup was not enough and had arranged for a Summer Cup to be competed for in the spring. The Old Firm declined, so the other sixteen sides were grouped geographically, and it must be admitted that Hibs were a shade fortunate to qualify, since they finished behind Hearts, level with Dunfermline and above only Falkirk. But Hearts were off on holiday to America, and Hibs beat Dunfermline to reach the semi-finals, and then beat Kilmarnock over two exciting games to qualify for the final.

That had to be held over until August because Aberdeen was in the grip of typhoid, so maybe there was something in the trophy's name, and the first leg was at Pittodrie. Hibs survived a pummelling to return home just one goal down, thanks largely to Scott's two equalisers. Even that deficit was all but too much, because there was not long to go in a tense second leg when Stan Vincent scored the first goal to take the tie into extra time. Eric Stevenson put Hibs ahead, and Hibs seemed to have pulled it off, but an unfortunate bounce of the ball gave Cooke a lucky last minute goal.

Aberdeen won the toss and chose Pittodrie, but with Hamilton crashing in an early goal and in general an inspiration, Hibs could afford the luxury of a missed penalty in an emphatic 3–1 win; Scott and Cormack were the other scorers. To put Hibs' win into perspective, they had won just six games out of twelve in a competition lacking the Old Firm, but a piece of silverware did wonders for the club's confidence, as was amply demonstrated a month later on October 7th.

Real Madrid

It was Hearts' turn to represent Edinburgh in the Fairs Cup, so Hibs brought, at great expense, Real Madrid to Easter Road. Hibs had to raise prices by half to meet their guarantee, on the assumption that about thirty thousand fans would be there. The Spaniards were a little past their best, although they were to win the European Cup again in 1966.

Thus far, Stein, like Galbraith, had tried in vain to blend the skills of Quinn and Hamilton into the same team, but this was the night it all came right. Quinn initiated moves from just in front of the back four, while Hamilton played further forward than usual, and completely eclipsed his much-vaunted opponents like Puskas. Cormack scored with a volley on the turn in twenty minutes to waken the Spaniards up, but as time went on and they tried to raise their game, they were matched at every move by a Hibs' team in which wing-halves Baxter and Stanton were outstanding. With six minutes remaining, Zoco deflected a Quinn free kick into his own net, and suddenly the game was beyond Real. Hibs carried on with the good work—and the green shorts that Real had insisted they wore—to Ibrox a few days later, where there was the famous pre-match discussion between Jim Baxter of Rangers and Hamilton about who was going to show whom what. Hibs won 4–2, and Hamilton won hands down.

Willie's Great Goal

Willie Hamilton scored a number of great goals in his spell at Easter Road, but the one which is best remembered was that at Tynecastle in the opening match of 1965. Hibs were part of a four horse race for the title which, unusually, did not involve either half of the Old Firm, but had yet to show they could handle Hearts on a regular basis. This time they held out during a hectic first half in which Hearts as usual started at a hundred miles an hour, and were still level at the interval. That was still the case with about twelve minutes remaining, when Quinn took a free kick to Hamilton on Hibs left. Hamilton seemed to have let the ball run too far so as to allow him only to get a cross in, but, ever in pursuit of the impossible, he struck a shot with such swerve and venom that it was in the roof of Cruikshank's net before the Hearts' goalkeeper could move.

Apart from being a brilliant goal, it gave Hibs an important win. They beat Rangers again, for their first league double since 1902–03, and might well have won the championship, had Jock Stein not resigned before that could happen to take over as manager of Celtic.

Bob Shankly

Bob Shankly from Dundee was Hibs next manager. He had built the exciting Dens Park side which had swept impressively to the 1962 league championship and then the European Cup semi-finals, but had been most unhappy about the subsequent break-up of that team. He was a traditionalist, a manager who liked his players to take responsibility and express themselves, rather like Ivan Golac without the comedy. Hibs had shown ambition in attracting some big name players and Jock Stein, but Shankly was to find the reality of that football life in Edinburgh was only different in degree from that in Dundee. If he had realised that, he might not have come.

Shankly took over as Hibs slipped out of contention for the 1965 championship; readers may recall Kilmarnock's last day jaunt to Tynecastle. there was another Summer Cup in the spring, and Hibs reached the final again only to lose to Motherwell in extra time.

The Hibs' side under Shankly had a settled look for the next four years or so, despite the constant rumours which linked Cormack's name with most of the sides south of Berwick. In fact, Cormack stayed longer than Shankly, despite a stream of his colleagues moving on.

In goal, Thomson Allan gradually took over from Willie Wilson; the fullbacks were Bobby Duncan, a converted inside forward until a crude tackle by John Hughes of Celtic more or less ended his career, and, with Parke unable to settle in Edinburgh, Joe Davis from Third Lanark made 273 consecutive appearances, and struck up a partnership with Eric Stevenson which brought the new Hibs captain forty-three goals. Between them, Pat Stanton developed into the best sweeper in the country alongside first McNamee and later John Madsen, a granite-like Dane Hibs signed from Morton.

Midfield duties fell mainly to Baxter, nearing the close of his playing days, Alan Cousin, a classy player Shankly brought from Dundee, and Allan McGraw, who had signed as a prolific striker with Morton. In attack, although Martin, Hamilton and Jim Scott went to England, Hibs remained a potent force with Cormack, Quinn, Stevenson, O'Rourke, the emerging Colin Stein and latterly the veteran Celtic sharpshooter Joe McBride and the precocious Peter Marinello.

Despite this array of talent, Hibs were not really ever in the hunt for honours. One reason was Celtic, whose football was of exhilirating attack, and another was Rangers, whose wasn't. Hibs-Celtic games tended to be classics with lots of goals, albeit mostly for Celtic and notably in the 1968 league cup final, where Hibs' two late goals only made it 6–2. Hibs tended to be at a disadvantage against hard-tackling teams like Rangers, and on heavy grounds, so that Dumbarton was a problem. However, their ascendancy over Hearts was a pleasing feature, and Hibs returned to Tynecastle in September 1965 and Stevenson and O'Rourke shared four goals in the opening ten minutes.

The lack of bite also told against Hibs in a number of European ties, despite some histrionic heroics by Peter Cormack in particular, and it was all the more surprising then that their outstanding result in the Shankly years should come against the Italian league leaders.

Napoli

Hibs had gone to Italy for the first leg and lost 4–1, so that, against top Italian opponents, the away goal looked likely to prove academic. Moreover, Harold Wilson had devalued sterling while they were there, so they could not even meet their hotel bill. When Napoli came to Easter Road in November 1967 therefore, the ground was less than half full. Despite that, it is hard to find Hibs' fans of that generation who do not claim to have been there. Those who were saw Hibs take the lead in only five minutes when goalkeeper Dino Zoff was completely taken unawares by a long long shot from Bobby Duncan which sailed in over his head. There was much effort, the usual cast-iron penalty claims disregarded and some near things but it was on the interval when Quinn squeezed in the second goal.

The tie turned on a single minute in the middle of the second half. Alex Scott, who had been bought from Everton after his brother had left Hibs, swung over two corners. Cormack rose spring-heeled to head home the first at the near post, Pat Stanton stooped to head the second one at the far post. Colin Stein added another near the end, and Hibs had incredibly won by 5–0.

Leeds United

Hibs reward was another big name, Don Revie's Leeds United. Hibs played well at Elland Road after losing a goal in four minutes, and did not lose any more. The second leg attracted forty thousand to Easter Road. Within six minutes of the start, Stein had got a toe to the ball to send it high into the net. Hibs continued to attack fervently, and in one break down the slope in the second half, managed a two on one situation but Stein shot weakly to waste the chance. Then with six minutes to go, the Hibs' goalkeeper was penalised for too many steps—maybe the twentieth like infringement of the game—and Giles took a quick free kick for Charlton to head home. The reader will appreciate that then Charlton was the England centre-half of 1966 fame and not the likeable Irish manager of later years, and so Hibs and the crowd were unhappy; Hibs were left to score twice and could not.

Colin Stein was the player who broke Shankly's heart. He eventually had to agree to Stein's going, and terms were agreed with Everton. Stein refused, and it became clear that he wanted only to go to Ibrox. Hibs received their first six figure cheque. Shankly resigned, but was persuaded to think again. He did, but stayed only until the following September, 1969. Hibs supporters never showed any signs of welcome to their erstwhile hero Stein when he returned to Easter Road.

Willie McFarlane

There were many applicants for the job, but Willie McFarlane the Hibs' full-back from the fifties, was the one who impressed the Hibs' chairman Harrower most, not least for his enthusiasm combined with the fact that as a company manager, he did not really need the money. McFarlane was boss of Stirling Albion at the time. He made an immediate impression by getting Cormack to sign another contract despite yet more transfer rumours.

For a few months all went well, with Marinello starring on the right wing in a way that impressed even Archie McPherson. Then at New Year, McFarlane announced that there was no truth in the rumour that Marinello was leaving, and twenty-four hours later, he was an Arsenal player. Cormack was frustrated, and was sent off against Hearts and again on his second game back from suspension. Hibs sold him to Nottingham Forest.

The same year Harrower, now seventy years of age, sold his holding in the club to Tom Hart, an East Lothian builder who had been keen for some time to buy Harrower out. Things were not so sweet between McFarlane and Hart as they had been with his predecessor, and they came to a head in December when the manager's team choice for a Fairs Cup game with Liverpool was overruled and McFarlane, a man of integrity, resigned.

Dave Ewing

Dave Ewing was an English coach whom apparently Hibs had been lucky to get. He was given the manager's job now, and lasted only until the end of the season. He had the team playing to a Leeds-like style completely foreign to Hibs players and supporters. In a rare moment of popularity he told the press that Rangers were rubbish, although Hibs had not actually beaten them. At the end of the season he went to a coaching job in England. His spell as manager laster only eight lines.

Eddie Turnbull

So within months of taking over, Tom Hart was on the lookout for a new manager. Eddie Turnbull had been a candidate for the job before, but the difference this time was that he and Hart were friends. Turnbull had built an Aberdeen team that had won the 1970 Scottish Cup and were now the only realistic challengers to Celtic. His health was suspect, he had a fine relationship with his assistant Jimmy Bonthrone. The choice was to leave what he had worked so well to build at Aberdeen to return to Easter Road where his heart lay from his playing

Alan Gordon in thoughtful mood

days. Turnbull decided to move. The modern adjective to describe this situation is Jeffriesque.

With all the chopping and changing, Turnbull's first season was one of settling down and team building. Bertie Auld came as a short-term measure on a free transfer from Celtic, and Jim Herriott, the Scotland international goalkeeper, from Birmingham, although he was actually playing in South Africa. Alex Edwards was signed from Dunfermline in October, and when Joe Baker's injury problems persisted, ex-Heart Alan Gordon was brought in to lead the line. The combination of Edwards' crosses, Gordon's heading ability and O'Rourke voracious feeding off the crumbs was to prove lethal. Pat Stanton was now captain and the rest of the team was generally the home grown talent of John Brownlie, John Blackley and Alex Cropley, together with earlier buys Arthur Duncan, Jim Black and Erich Schaedler, whom McFarlane had brought with him from Stirling.

Hibs got off to a moderate start, but performances improved, and they only lost three goals once, against Airdrie, before they reached the 1972 cup final. A final with Celtic had probably come too early for the new Hibs, and it showed. They lost a goal in two minutes, and six in all, and the feature which was to haunt most Hibs-Celtic games for the next few years was the ability of Deans, by no means a great centre, to score against Jim Black. Deans scored three in that final.

The Drybrough Cup

It was a black afternoon, but Hibs bounced back at the start of the new season, having qualified as one of the First division's top four scorers for the Drybrough Cup. Their confidence would not have been harmed by their effortless demolition of Rangers by 3–0 in the semi-final, and so after just three months they were back at Hampden to face Celtic again.

This time it was different, and early in the second half, Hibs led by three goals, at which point some Celtic supporters took to the field and held up proceedings for twenty minutes or so; this obviously had the desired effect, as Hibs pattern deserted them, and by the end of ninety minutes it was 3–3. Then in injury time, O'Rourke, on as a substitute, drove high into the net from twenty yards, and in the final minute, Arthur Duncan, apparently just passing the last seconds on the wing, suddenly took off, left McGrain for dead, and from an acute angle rifled the ball inside the far post to make sure of victory. It was not often that Celtic under Stein lost five goals.

The League Cup

When Hibs' supporters talk of 'the great team of the early seventies', as regularly reported in the SoS Sports Diary, it is the autumn of 1972 that they are remembering, as Hibs swept to their league cup triumph, quarter-finals of the European Cupwinners Cup and, at New Year, the top of the league, in dramatic fashion.

The league cup section matches were low key, with two to qualify from Hibs, Aberdeen, Queens Park and Queen of the South; the fun started in the knockout stages quarter-final at Tannadice, where Hibs were behind at half-time but scored five in the second period to make the second leg a formality. Much the same thing happened at Broomfield in the next round. Hibs trailed by a goal at half-time; O'Rourke equalised from a penalty only for Hibs to lose a similar goal a minute later, but they went on to score another five, including a hat-trick from Duncan. One of John Brownlie's many cantrips into Rangers' penalty area ended with him scoring the only goal in the Hampden semi-final, and Hibs were poised to take on Celtic again.

After the two previous finals, the first hour of this one was largely cat and mouse, but the key issue was that Hibs were dominating midfield, where Stanton was immense.It was the Hibs' skipper who broke the deadlock on the hour, taking a chipped free kick from Edwards and driving home, and minutes later flighting a perfect cross for O'Rourke to head home at the near post. McNeill knew little about his block on the line from Gordon, and Stanton hit the post as Hibs tried to finish it off, but although the only further score came from Dalgleish, Hibs had won well.

Sporting Lisbon

Hibs' reward for their spring outing to Hampden was a place in the Cupwinners' Cup, and their first opponents were Besa from Albania, who lost seven goals at Easter Road in a complete mismatch. The second round was tougher, against Sporting Lisbon, and despite one

John Brounlie celebrates one of his goals in Hibs 6–2 League Cup win at Airdrie

of their best performances in their first appearance in purple, Hibs lost 2–1 in Portugal. They struggled in the first half at Easter Road to break down a very competent-looking defence, and at half-time were only level at one apiece, having lost the important away goal. The second half was a different story, with another five goals down the slope, as well as a thunderbolt from Brownlie off the post. O'Rourke had a hat-trick this time, one of six he scored during the season.

Hibs were also going strong in the league, scored eight goals against Ayr United when they displayed the league cup, and then for once were disappointed only to draw at Parkhead when a win was expected. So they remained two points behind Celtic at the turn of the year, and when the Old Firm game was cancelled had therefore a chance to go top—if they could beat Hearts at Tynecastle by six goals.

It seemed improbable, but they went one better. Park missed one early chance for Hearts, but them Hibs created mayhem in the Tynecastle defence, scoring five times at the Gorgie Road end. O'Rourke volleyed in the first from close range, Gordon placed a neat shot past Garland as he slipped for the second and Duncan ran clear of the defence to score a third. A volley from Cropley and a header from Duncan each went in off Garland's right-hand post to make it five. O'Rourke missed from six yards after Edwards had caught the defenders cold with a clever free kick, and the score would certainly have been higer if the aim latterly had not been to make sure Edwards got a goal. O'Rourke and Gordon scored in the second half of an historic game.

Suddenly that was that. The following Saturday, John Brownlie broke his leg and was out for a year, and Alex Edwards incurred an eight week suspension for accumulated misdoings. Hibs league challenge faltered, they went out of the Cupwinners' Cup to what is now the Croatian side Hajduk Split, and lost to Rangers in the cup, after seeming to have done the hard bit by drawing at Ibrox.

By August 1973, Des Bremner had successfully installed himself in Brownlie's place, and Tony Higgins and Bobby Smith were playing in most first team games. Hibs had qualified for the Drybrough Cup again, and they won it again, though in less style—they needed extra time to beat Rangers in the semi-final this time, and also to account

Left. Pat Stanton
Right. Ally McLeod beats Rangers' Colin Jackson

for Celtic in the final. Indeed it was in the last minute of the extra half hour that Alan Gordon opened and finished the scoring.

There was also less style about their early league play, especially the 4–1 defeat at Tynecastle, Hibs' first league defeat there since September 1963. However, by Christmas they were second in the table and had been unlucky not to beat Leeds in another intense UEFA Cup tie—especially the first leg at Leeds where Stanton ruled in midfield and Higgins was a relevation up front. Both legs were goalless, and Pat Stanton hit the post to contribute the only miss in the penalty shootout.

Hibs stayed on to finish second to Celtic again, and made another one big push to get upsides with the Glasgow side. They signed Joe Harper, who had scored a lot of goals for Turnbull at Aberdeen, from Everton for a club record fee of £120,000. The sad fact was that Harper's signing did not pay a dividend; the goals did not come as often as they should, the supporters never took to a player who had been far from popular at Easter Road while with Aberdeen, and Jimmy O'Rourke, now considered surplus to requirements, went to St Johnstone.

The Black Week in October

However, in 1974, it seemed that Hibs just might finally topple Celtic, and certainly by October they had suffered only one defeat—to an O'Rourke goal for St Johnstone. Then in the space of seven days, these dreams were shattered. Hibs lost 5–0 at Parkhead in a league match, and then took on Juventus in the UEFA Cup at Easter Road. What had the possibility of being another European glory night when they came back from a goal down to take the lead turned sour when, going for the bigger lead they would certainly need in Turin, they were caught on the break—three times—and lost 4–2. Then on the Saturday Celtic beat them 6–3 in the league cup final, with another hat-trick for Deans against Black.

More bad news was to follow. Alex Cropley was sold to Arsenal to balance the books over the Harper affair, with Ally McLeod coming from Southampton for £25,000 to replace him. There was also a change in sentiment by the manager. Playing exciting attacking football was all very well, but they still lost too many goals to Celtic, and there was also the Premier League in prospect. Turnbull decided Hibs would have to be harder, and signed Roy Barry from Crystal Palace. He had been with Hearts and Dunfermline earlier but always wanted to play for Hibs. Certainly when Hibs met Celtic again, Deans physical style cut no ice with Barry and Hibs won 2–1, but a great era was over.

— 9 —

THE PREMIER LEAGUE

The Premier League was to be the salvation of Scottish football; with the top sides playing each other every week instead of the Airdries and St Mirrens of this world, they would learn the concentration and streetwiseness without which too many Scottish sides at national and club level had succumbed to patently inferior opposition, particularly by losing 'silly' goals. This new system has been in place now for twenty years, and at the time of writing, Motherwell have just been beaten by Myllykofken Palo-47, a year after Aberdeen lost to Skonto Riga.

The year 1975 also marked Hibs centenary, and for the supporters at least, the main attraction was the game against Derby County, the English champions, to mark the occasion. The game itself was unremarkable, with Derby raising their game in the second half long enough to score the only goal before going back to sleep again. For those more closely associated with the club through the years, there was also a large reception in October, and among those present were Willie Harper and Jimmy McColl from the Hibs' team of the twenties, and Pat Stanton who was not only current captain, but related to the very first Hibs' skipper, Michael Whelehan.

Hibs were obviously in favour of the Premier League—chairman Tom Hart along with Rangers' Willie Waddell were the men behind its inception. Jim McLean of Dundee United on the other hand railed against the Premier League from its inception, as he did about many things, but certainly in its first season, it seemed to prove its critics wrong. By the halfway point, nine of the ten sided had formed into two tight groups. At the top, a single point at times separated Celtic, Rangers, Hibs and Motherwell, while Aberdeen, Hearts and Dundee United contested the second relegation place, rather as in 1995, but on the earlier occasion with Ayr United and Dundee. It was Dundee who lost out on the last day to go down with the long since doomed St Johnstone.

Hibs saw off Motherwell's challenge but then faded themselves towards the end, and by the final day were happy enough to pip the Fir Park side for third position and a place in Europe. In an effort to boost their defence, they bought the ex-Clydebank goalkeeper, Mike McDonald, from Stoke City, where he had understudied Shilton and Banks, but with Jim McArthur already on the staff, one wondered whether that was the area most in need of improvement.

With Ally McLeod injured for most of the season, Pat Stanton played further forward still, and headed several important goals for Hibs, notably a last-gasp equaliser at Tynecastle and a double to beat Rangers at Easter Road. However, Hibs lost at Montrose in the league cup, Stanton was one of the casualties, and manager Turnbull did not seem to remember that Stanton was still one of the best defenders in Britain when, just one week later, Hibs set out to defend a slender 1–0 lead against Liverpool at Anfield with Stanton on the bench. Liverpool won 3–1.

Towards the end of the season, there was further transfer activity—Harper went back to Aberdeen where he was more appreciated. The transfer fee was only a quarter of what Hibs had paid Everton. To replace him, Hibs signed two Rangers non-regulars, Ally Scott and Graeme Fyfe, the former a centre, and their goalscoring problems really started. To make matters worse, left-back Iain Munro went to Ibrox and later played for Scotland.

Unfortunately, the euphoria of that first season did not endure, at least not for Hibs' fans. There is a school of thought that Hibs were in decline from the break-up of the league cupwinning eleven, but the statistics do not back that up. In the first ten years of the premier league, Hibs averaged better than seventh position, which was better than the previous twenty years, and their position during the second decade of the new set-up has shown a modest improvement on that. There are a number of factors which produced the 'feel-bad' effect. Firstly, Hibs hit a chronic goalscoring shortage at the same time as the number of goals per game in the Premier League fell much below the number in the old First Division. Secondly, a team in sixth/seventh position in an eighteen team First Division can be expected to win more games than it loses; the reverse is true for a team in the same position in a ten team Premier League. And thirdly, the lack of goals and goalmouth incident was not helped by the methods adopted by some sides, especially away from home, and notably Dundee United under Jim McLean and Partick Thistle under Bertie Auld. In 1976–77, Hibs' four games against Aberdeen failed to produce a single goal.

Season 1976–77 showed above all that Hibs had been walking a tightrope. Having lost Harper, Pat Stanton, now certainly approaching veteran stage, was seen by Celtic as the answer to their problem in defence, where Stanton was happiest. Hibs got the young Jackie McNamara in exchange, and it proved a good one for Hibs in that Stanton was to call it a day little more than a year later, while McNamara was to give Hibs good service for a decade, and especially at sweeper after John Blackley joined Newcastle a year later. The goalscoring problems were chronic, especially with the talented McLeod on the sidelines. In the league, they managed less than a goal a game, and Scott at centre amassed three. Hibs' first home win did not come until Christmas Eve, a 1–0 win against Ayr United at Easter Road in front of a small, wearily tolerant crowd, and courtesy of an own goal. The one goal barrier was not broken until March when Hibs scored twice against Kilmarnock. There was also a UEFA Cup defeat from Oesters Vaxjo, somewhere in central Scandinavia to contend with, so the benefits of the Premier League were clearly still to be seen.

On the other hand, bolstered by George Stewart, a Hibs fanatic and friend of O'Rourke and Stanton, Hibs' defence was just as parsimonious as their opponents', and Hibs finished sixth, seven points above Hearts who were relegated—that showed how important were the seven points Hibs took from Hearts, much the same as in some of the recent seasons during Hearts' recently ended spell of dominance. Since Hibs drew fully half of their thirty-six league matches, it was not surprising that they did not beat anyone else three times.

Further moves were made the following autumn to solve the striking problem, although not anything that costed money. Jim McKay of Brora seemed to have some potential, and came to Easter Road on a month's trial. One stumbling block seemed to be Brora's wanting a £10,000 transfer fee, at the same time as Hibs received a six-figure fee for Blackley. Martin Henderson came on loan from Rangers but his only scoring contribution came in an Anglo-Scottish

Cup match against Bristol City. Then Bobby Hutchinson came from Dundee, and he made sufficient difference that Hibs' league tally finished fifty per cent above the year before, and they even pipped Celtic for the last European place. Unfortunately, Erich Schaedler went to Dens in return for Hutchinson, which meant former top scorer Bobby Smith filling in at left-back.

The Anglo-Scottish Cup was for the also-rans in England and Scotland, and this was the only occasion when Hibs reached the second round and met English opposition (In 1979–80, they lost to Ayr in the first round, a new low). They beat Blackburn Rovers home and away, an easier task then than now, and then met Bristol City. The first leg was at Easter Road, finished one apiece, and featured the sendings-off of Peter Cormack and ex-Leeds hatchet man Norman Hunter. Tom Hart called Bristol City butchers and refused to go to Bristol, but was persuaded to change his mind, and Hibs lost 5–3 at Ashton Gate. The new-found professionalism came through in that Hibs apparently did not know that their white shorts would not be allowed since City wore white shorts too, and had to borrow black ones once at Bristol.

That was only the start as far as colour problems went. Hibs were the first club to attract shirt sponsorship, from the sportswear firm Bukta. The problems started when Hibs were due to appear on television—the TV companies would not show shirts with 'Bukta' written on them. One would have thought that the TV exposure would have been a major factor in the deal, but Bukta agreed that Hibs should wear a different non-Bukta strip on these occasions, stipulating only that it should not be the green and white which was associated with their name.

The change strip was a truly dreadful outfit in purple with green and yellow down the white sleeves, and Hibs were seen in it losing to Celtic in Glasgow and to Ayr United at home—since it was the first post-war home defeat by Ayr, that did not improve the general feeling much. Also, since purple was in between red and blue, it was not appropriate against Rangers, Hearts, Aberdeen etc., most of the sides Hibs might have been expected to be on TV against.

The answer to this one was a strip of plain yellow jerseys like goalkeepers in the fifties, and Hibs first tried them out against Rangers. They therefore became the first side to have three different strips at the same time, although unlike the present-day fashion among the so-called bigger clubs, the object was not to rip off young supporters and their parents.

This fiasco reached a conclusion at a cup-tie against East Fife at Easter Road. It will be readily believed that this was not the intended television treat, but the weather made it the only one. Unfortunately, Hibs were due to wear the Bukta strips, and the purple togs were not to be found. Eventually, Bukta agreed to Hibs wearing a pre-sponsorship set of green and white jerseys, and the teams appeared nearly half an hour late once the television moguls were happy. What they did not know, apparently, was that East Fife also had sponsors, and they were allowed to play in their normal shirts with the sponsors' logo on them.

The Norwegians

In 1978–79, the interest was again largely off the field rather than on it, despite Hibs playing in Europe, and reaching the semi-finals of the league cup and the final of the Scottish Cup. With a string of professionally uninteresting performances, they were the last team to remain unbeaten, and reached the second round of the UEFA Cup after a stifling performance in Gotherburg. At that point they ran into Racing Strasbourg, who had more flair than Hibs had encountered for a year or two, and the classy French side won more easily than the 2–1 aggregate would suggest.

The off-field activity, or lack of it, centred round Hibs' attempt to sign two Norwegians, Svein Mathisen and Izaak Refvik, and to break through the red tape which prevented them taking much part. They did play in an exciting league cup quarter final against Morton; Hibs had lost by one goal at Greenock thanks to some heavy tackling, and Refvik, a tiny figure but with a lot of pace, scored both goals to take Hibs through. Even then, they had to hold their breath as Morton's Ritchie put a penalty over the bar. That game also gave ex-Heart Ralph Callachan, whom Hibs had swapped John Brownlie for with Newcastle, one of his best games for Hibs. The semi-final at Dens against Aberdeen laboured predictably into extra time, and the deadlock was only broken when McDonald misjudged a high ball which went in off his post. This effectively ended McDonald's run in Hibs' goal and Jim McArthur emerged from years in the reserves to take over.

The position of the Norwegians was finally sorted out long after their trial periods of three months was over and they had left these shores. Only full internationalists would be allowed work permits. Had this been implemented earlier, Refvik would not have been able to play, as he had only played at under-21 level, while Mathiesen, who was a full cap, could have played, but in fact did not get into the Hibs' team anyway.

It was a measure of the attractiveness of the fixture, and, admittedly, the weather, that when Hibs met Aberdeen in another cup-tie, this time the Scottish Cup semi at Hampden, fewer than ten thousand spectators were there. McLeod scored twice and Hibs won 2–1. The final was against Rangers at the same venue, and was another yawn, as Hibs played so very cautiously, to dampen any enthusiasm that the big Rangers' support in particular could raise. It was only in the last few minutes that they had a go, and a shot from Colin Campbell almost did the trick, but McCloy saved well and so it was back to Hampden for a replay.

That was neither a lot better, not any more conclusive—it just went on half an hour longer, but at last the third game produced a game worthy of the occasion. Higgins and Johnstone had first half goals courtesy of goalkeeping errors, and in the second, Johnstone scored again, and Mcleod did likewise from the penalty spot when Jackson brought Hutchinson down. Into extra time, and Alex Miller did his first good act for Hibs by missing a penalty, only for Arthur Duncan, racing back to clear, to head a high cross into his own net to give Rangers the trophy.

George Best

One feature about the Premier League was the number of close and drawn games. One corollary of that was that if a team became stranded at the foot of the table by just a few points, then the proportion of points that they would need from the rest of the programme would normally guarantee a European place. That was exactly the position that Hibs found themselves in in the autumn of 1979, and, not having the players to make a run for Europe, they never looked like closing the gap. Selling the industrious Des Bremner to Aston Villa, and taking striker Joe Ward, who scored no goals at all for Hibs, in part exchange, did not help, but what would have been a season of complete misery was only lightened by the arrival of George Best in December.

George Best was a diversion in an otherwise gloomy time. He played twenty-two games for Hibs, scored four goals, missed the odd game for his own reasons, and incurred one suspension for doing so. On the other hand he boosted attendances so that he more than repaid the rumoured £2000 per game that the Hibs' chairman was paying him, and he still showed a degree of skill which was absent from the increasingly sterile Premier League. There was never any chance of his steering Hibs out of trouble, but he did manage to play in a Scottish Cup semi-final, against Celtic, in which Hibs lost 5–0.

Eddie Turnbull had by now lost the star status that he had been accorded when Hibs won the league cup. More recently, his health had been a problem, his team selections were sometimes baffling, and he was supposed to be grooming a successor. It was no surprise when he resigned after the cup defeat. Willie Ormond, who had been assisting Turnbull, took over. At least he had a lot of First Division experience, as he had been manager of Hearts. Unfortunately, Ormond had personal and health problems which precluded his giving the Hibs' job the dedication and focus it needed, and he stayed only a few months.

The First Division

There was little doubt that Hibs would come straight back up. With players like McLeod, Callachan, and at times the returned Peter Cormack and John Connelly, ex-St Johnstone and Everton, they had too much ability for most of their opponents, and the additional space and time to exploit it. They lost the opening game against Raith Rovers, but were in command from the week in October whn they beat potential rivals Dundee, Motherwell and Ayr United in the space of eight days.

When Willie Ormond retired, Hibs brought Bertie Auld from Partick Thistle, certainly the manager with the best credentials for fighting the battles to stay up in the years to come. Auld's style was not to everyone's liking—in fact to practically nobody's—but Hibs continued to pick up the points in low scoring games, losing very few goals, and clinched the championship by beating Raith Rovers on a sunny spring afternoon at Easter Road.

Two brighter features of these times at easter Road were the installation of an early electronic scoreboard, which worked fitfully for a while before being damaged in a storm, and, more successfully the first undersoil heating in Scotland. This was a sound investment, especially as it was mostly paid off in one go when Manchester United, short of match practice, came north on boxing day. The score was 1–1, and Hibs' goal came from Willie Jamieson, another striker who was to find goals hard to get in the top flight.

There were not many youngsters coming through at Easter Road—Craig Paterson, Gordon Rae and Ally Brazil were the pick—and so Auld paid around £60,000 for each of Alan Sneddon from Celtic, who was to give excellent service for several years, and Gary Murray from Montrose, who looked the part but found himself out of his depth in the Premier League.

Nevertheless, Hibs were harder to beat than before, even if they had to suffer opposing fans' taunts of 'Partick Thistle football'—they knew how to hurt! However, they finished sixth, just one point adrift of St Mirren who qualified for Europe. More importantly, Hibs lost their chairman—Tom Hart collapsed at Pittodrie and died later.

Kenny Waugh

The transition between Hart and his successor went smoothly; Kenny Waugh, ex-engineer and now successful bookmaker, had already reached an understanding with Hart to buy his interest in the club, and Hart's unfortunate death just brought the transaction forward. The loser was Bertie Auld. Waugh liked neither the style of play which Auld's teams played, nor indeed the salary which the fans were not coming in large numbers to pay for. One league cup match at Easter Road was watched by only two thousand.At the end of a league cup section which Hibs had conceded to Rangers even before the final defeat at Airdrie, Auld and his assistant Pat Quinn were out of work.

Waugh knew exactly who the fans would want at Easter Road, and in no time Pat Stanton was installed with Jimmy O'Rourke and George Stewart as assistants. Stanton had earned top marks while assisting Alex Ferguson at Aberdeen and then taken just five months at Cowdenbeath to convince Dunfermline to give him the East End job.

It was not an easy start. Craig Paterson had gone to Ibrox, to help balance the books and because he was determined to go anyway, and the league was due to start at once. Hibs failed to win any of their first six matches, and then beat lowly Motherwell by the only goal. They did not win again until they beat Motherwell by the only goal again on the next round of matches. Moreover, Jim McArthur was injured at Ibrox, and, now Hibs only experienced goalkeeper, tried to carry on, but clearly was not fit. Something had to be done, and it was. Hibs signed Alan Rough from Partick, whom he had kept in the Premier League more or less single-handed. His role at Easter Road seemed little different.

Stanton also bought Mike Conroy from Celtic, where he did not command a regular first team place; he didn't at Easter Road either, but the same could not be said of Willie Irvine, from Motherwell, a striker noted for spectacular goals. The moves did the trick—Hibs only lost to Celtic and Aberdeen in a three month spell, and in a mad ninety minutes scored eight goals against Kilmarnock, who went down with Morton. The two goals which followed in the last seven games was what we were used to.

O'Rourke and Stewart left at the end of the season, to be replaced by another favourite, John Blackley, not only as assistant manager, but also a stop-gap sweeper, and he had an impressive second debut at Ibrox. In addition, Stanton was reaping the benefits of Bertie Auld's youth policy—he was one of the instigators of the Professional Youth League—with players like Brian Rice, Kevin McKee, Paul Kane and Mickey Weir coming through. He also signed ex-Morton forward Bobby Thompson from Middlesbro'. Thompson and Irvine struck a devastating partnership, and when Irvine scored against Hearts at New Year, it was his twentieth of the season.

Then Thompson stupidly pushed a referee in a game against St. Johnstone, received a six month suspension, so that Irvine's goals dried up, Thompson failed to regain his place, Alan Rough broke a bone in a foot as Hibs went out of the cup at Methil, and Hibs finished seventh after a start with so much promise, and Hearts made the last Europlace. On a sad note, Arthur Duncan was freed, and left the field as a Hib for the last time with a broken collarbone in a game against Meadowbank.

Season 1984–85 did not even have the bright start. Early defeats by Hearts and Meadowbank Thistle set the tone. McKee was attacked by a Rangers' fan at Ibrox, and Stanton was sent from the bench at Pittodrie for questioning an offside decision which TV evidence showed was indeed incorrect. The next home game was against Dumbarton, and seemed critical even so early, and the Sons scored three goals in quick succession to win 3–1. Stanton resigned, and was fined £500 for his remarks to the referee at Aberdeen, while the Ibrox ruffian had to pay just £100.

John Blackley took temporary charge, and impressed enough to be given the permanent position. Tommy Craig, player-manager of Carlisle, came in the same joint roles as Blackley had, and provided a pleasant touch of subtlety. Time was against Blackley, but he got off to a good start by signing Gordon Durie from East Fife for £70,000, and he made an immediate impact with two goals to draw at Dumbarton—still Hibs' main rivals for the dreaded tenth position.

By early January, Hibs were five points adrift of Dumbarton, and their manager, ex-Ranger Davy Wilson, seemed to think it was all over. But on the 12th of that month, Hibs got a break at last—they won at Ibrox, with a late winner from Colin Harris, who had come from Dundee. Hibs beat Dumbarton in a vital clash at Easter Road, and then scored five against Morton to be level on points with Dumbarton. They actually overtook the Boghead club on goal difference while both clubs were losing, and then won by a Paul Kane goal at Parkhead, a result which must have seemed a mortal blow at Dumbarton. When the crunch came, early goals from Rice and Irvine gave Hibs a 2–0 win at Boghead, and Hibs were effectively home and just about dry. Hibs took seventeen points from their last sixteen games, a percentage which over the whole season would have achieved a European place, but as it was they were happy enough to have daylight between them and Dumbarton.

— 10 —

HEADING FOR TROUBLE

Manager Blackley still did not have money to spend, at least not until Brian Rice decided to go to Nottingham Forest. Brian Clough offered £75,000, and so it went to a tribunal which awarded Hibs £175,000. About a quarter of that had been spent on bringing Steve Cowan, a striker, from Aberdeen, and he quickly built up a good understanding with Durie, at least midweek.

On Saturdays, Hibs lost their opening six league games. When Rangers won at Easter Road, the game started half an hour late because of the break-in by Glasgow fans to the North Stand and Albion Road end. When Hibs lost at Tynecastle by 2–1, their bad luck was 'about eleven on a scale of ten and drifting'. Their first win, at the seventh attempt was by a single goal scored by Ally Brazil against Motherwell.

It was all so different midweek. Cowan scored a hat-trick in the first league cup tie against Cowdenbeath in a 6–0 win. Motherwell scarcely fared batter a week later—Hibs scored six in a thirty minute spell either side of half-time to win 6–1, with a hat-trick by Durie this time. And the next game was really one to remember. Hibs met Celtic at Easter Road, and after extra time, the score was four apiece. Both sides had led twice, and in no case did the lead last more than a few minutes. A penalty decider was needed, and it was Pearce O'Leary who made the vital mistake, so let Hibs through to the semi-finals. Just to demonstrate what a difference a day makes, Hibs lost to the same opponents at the same venue by 5–0 in the league on the following Saturday.

The semi-finals were two-legged affairs. Gordon Chisholm had been signed from Sunderland by the time Rangers played the first game at Easter Road. He and Durie were the influential players as well as the scorers in a well-earned 2–0 win. The second leg was largely a case of Hibs holding out, but the only time their colours were lowered was by a typically unsaveable Davie Cooper free kick, so that Hibs were Hampden bound. But before they got there they did their confidence no harm at all by beating Rangers again, at Ibrox.

Aberdeen were arguably a better team than either Rangers or Celtic at the time, and they certainly showed it in the final. Eric Black and Stark had them two up, and the cup won, inside twelve minutes, and Black added a third later on to make certain. It had been a good effort to reach the final, and at least, as the Hibs support sang happily to the Hearts fans a week later, we were there. That was a game memorable mainly for Sandy Clark of Hearts missing from six yards after Alan Rough had fallen in the mud.

Christmas time was not especially festive. On the preceding Saturday, the Hibs-Rangers game was interrupted by a Rangers' supporter assaulting Alan Rough on the pitch because, as he explained to the court later, his girlfriend was pregnant, and then came the sad news of the death of Erich Schaedler. New Year brought little more cheer—Hearts' 3–1 Ne'erday win was their biggest in the Premier League against Hibs, and it was followed by Clydebank's second away win, 3–2 at Easter Road. Still, there was the cup to come, and to make sure, Hibs avoided playing on Saturdays for the first two rounds.

The first two ties were both at home on Sundays, and Hibs beat Dunfermline by 2–0, and then Ayr United by a single goal, and that came from Eddie May in injury time. Nobody thought they would see another classic between Hibs and Celtic like the league cup match earlier, but they came close in the quarter-final at Easter Road. With a quarter of an hour to go, it had been a good game, if nothing exceptional, and Celtic led 2–1. Then Chisholm headed in a Tortolano corner to equalise. Seven minutes lates, May was tripped, and Cowan slotted home the penalty, but before the cheering had ceased the referee decided that Fulton had impeded Mo Johnston in some way, and McClair scored from the spot. There was still more to come, because in the dying seconds Hibs' substitutes Harris and May combined for the latter to flick the ball home with his head for Hibs' first Cup win against Celtic since the 1902 final.

The rest of the season was somewhat inconsequential. Aberdeen beat Hibs 3–0 in the semi-final at Dens Park, and accounted for Hearts by the same score in the final, in a game remarkably similar to the league cup final inasmuch as Aberdeen had it all wrapped up within the first few minutes. Gordon Durie remained ambitious/unsatisfied and went to Chelsea for £400,000, and Hibs' supporters watched the season draw to a close on a lazy summer's afternoon watching Dundee United win at Easter Road and listening to the Dundee v Hearts radio commentary from Dens Park.

Gordon Durie was a player that Hibs did not want to lose, but his transfer brought the wherewithal to strengthen the pool, and over the summer, they made five new signings. The Dundee United pair, Billy Kirkwood and Stewart Beedie, had the necessary experience, and the former took over the captaincy. George McCluskey, ex-Celtic and even more experienced but even less speedy than of yore came on a free transfer from Leeds, and Hibs signed the young Stirling Albion player Willie Irvine. But the most exotic deal was concluded in Albequerche in New Mexico where the Northern Ireland world cup party was based, and where Linfield forward Mark Caughey joined Hibs.

The new men had something to prove when the new season kicked off in August, and the same could be said for Rangers, who had new player/manager Graeme Souness and his first three big-name English signings, Woods, Butcher and West on show when the two met in the opening fixture at Easter Road. Few will forget the spectacle of Sounness ignominiously being given his marching orders before half-time of his Premier League debut for a horrific tackle which left George McCluskey with a hole in his leg, an act only marginally more serious than the tackle on Billy Kirkwood for which had Sounness had already been booked. There was a general melée, as a result of which nearly all the players had an extra two disciplinary points added to their record. A few Hibs players won appeals against that on the grounds of being uninvolved (Weir), unconscious (Fulton) or too badly hurt to take any part (McCluskey).Hibs won 2–1.

Unfortunately, Hibs were unable to carry that spirit and determination on; in particular, despite some nice touches and a turn of speed, Mark Caughey was not a success, and later in the season he went to Hamilton; likewise, young Irvine failed to deliver the promise which Blackley had seen in him. Hibs gravitated again toward the danger area, and failed to win another league game until the last two in the first quarter, against strugglers Clydebank and Hamilton. At least with these two in the division, there was every chance that Hibs would stay up, especially Hamilton, but in the second meeting with Hibs, the Douglas Park team scored their first league win in seventeen starts, and an easy one it was, with Collins' late goal for Hibs only making it 3–1.

John Blackley was not there to see it; a few games earlier, Hibs had won only one of their second series of matches, by a single goal against Falkirk. There followed another dire performance and a 3–1 defeat at Paisley, and Blackley resigned. His assistant Tommy Craig took over temporarily, and was in charge in, among others, the game against Hamilton. By the time Rangers came to Easter Road in early December to start the second half of the campaign, Hibs had Alex Miller in place.

Alex Miller

Miller had taken St Mirren to their 1987 Scottish Cup win, with a young team which he had largely built, and although his playing career had been with Rangers, his commitment to Hibs since his appointment has been such that his former employment is no longer an issue even to the most prejudiced of Hibs' supporters. He did not get off to the best of starts; although Hibs held Rangers to a scoreless draw, Hibs reached New Year without a further win.

With the prospect of another derby against Hearts coming up, Miller went into the transfer market on Hogmanay, and in a triple swoop, brought Graeme Mitchell, captain and versatile defender from Hamilton, Dougie Bell from Rangers and Tom McIntyre, Aberdeen's centre-half who has since shown a remarkable ability to keep Mark Hateley of Rangers under control. Mark Fulton went to Hamilton as part of the transactions. Unfortunately the derby was cancelled, but the new-look side got off to a good start by winning 3–1 at Brockville, with Bell amongst the scorers.

With a new manager and players, it was refreshing to see Hibs have a go at Hearts in the rearranged derby without the signs of mental block which seemed to have afflicted them in these games for some time. McCluskey gave them an early lead, and by the interval, with Bell running the show in midfield, Hibs might have been four up. In fact, it took a goal from Weir near half-time to bring them level, after

Colquhoun had hit two goals of the speculative variety from outside the penalty area which go in once in a million.

After all their good work, therefore, Hibs finished the game holding out for a draw, but commentators were noting that they were playing in a more organised way and were becoming harder to beat. They lost at Clydebank in a disappointing cup-tie, especially as Hibs had scored four times against the same opponents in the second half of a league game a week earlier, but in their final round of eleven league games, they only lost four, finishing with a very youthful side indeed winning at Kilbowie.

By the autumn, all the talk was of the club takeover by David Duff, but Hibs did beat Rangers again at the start of the season only to lose faith with the fans three days later when they lost four goals in the first half at home to Dundee. But Neil Orr arrived from West Ham, which seemed to indicate serious intent and available funds, and Orr even scored on his debut in an entertaining league cup tie, which Hibs won 3–1, against Queen of the South. Everyone seemed to accept that Hibs were unlucky to go out of that competition when Rough was taken out in mid-air prior to the only goal at Fir Park, but Hibs were averaging a point a game, and relegation fears seemed to be banished for the time being.

Mickey Weir, out of contract, stated categorically that Hibs were nevertheless the only club for him, and immediately signed for Luton, but Hibs went into the market again and agreed terms, £250,000, with Leicester for Ian Andrews, England's Under-21 international. It was Andrews who turned down the move, but Hibs' loss was nothing to that of Celtic, who paid a lot of money for a short and disastrous spell of Andrews' goalkeeping. Instead, Hibs paid Oldham £325,000 for Andy Goram, who made his initial appearance against Dunfermline where the new man had little to do and Hibs overran the Fifers 4–0.

Gas before Calor

The high fences round the pitch were still in place in 1987, because English fans were liable to cause trouble, and the only real test of their efficacy came in November, during a game against Celtic. A US made gas canister, usually used for riot control, had exactly the opposite effect when thrown from the visitors' terracing on to the main covered terracing. Panic ensued, and the general stampede away from the gas was to a great extent impeded by the fences. The gates on to the pitch were not opened for some minutes because the cause of the trouble was not realised by those on the pitch. The result was nearly a hundred and fifty casualties. The person who was responsible got four years.

In the new year, Mickey Weir showed that he had been telling the truth by coming back to Hibs after just four months away, and in March, Gareth Evans came from Rotherham, and was an instant hit, by scoring within about twenty minutes of coming on as a substitute for Eddie May against Dundee at Easter Road. Gareth was not the complete answer to the goalscoring problem however, and as the season wound its way on, Hibs were destined for a mid-table position, and only Andy Goram had any cause to remember it. Firstly, he choked on his tongue at Ibrox, and, clearly in distress, could have died in the nearly four minutes that followed before referee Syme finally allowed treatment once the ball was in Hibs' net. On a happier note, Goram finished the season by scoring with a kick-out against Morton at Easter Road. Still, Hibs had taken three points from Ibrox, the same from Pittodrie, and four from Tannadice; they had also shared the eight points with Hearts equally, so that, while clearly the other side of the same story was poorer results against poorer teams, they seemed at last a match for anyone on their day.

Hibs' continued search for a strike force took them to even more exotic places than Rotherham, namely Eindhoven (if only just) and Barcelona. Bobby McDonald from PSV played with Hibs on their pre-season tour at Bury, but did not impress nearly enough to justify a £450,000 price tag. Steve Archibald on the other hand, whose transfer value had increased to £1.3m when he went to Barcelona, was now available to Hibs on a free transfer and his not inconsiderable personal terms, and turned out for Hibs in their opening league cup tie against Stranraer. Hibs' ambition was apparently a factor in Archibald's choice, the talk now was of a share flotation, and there was still a feel-good factor around Easter Road.

Hibs started off season 1988–89 even better than the previous one, unbeaten in eight league games although Aberdeen had put them out of the league cup in extra time. They also won at Tynecastle for the first time in a long time, despite Rae being sent off after just fifteen minutes, with Archibald scoring the second and decisive goal with a marvellous shot on the drop as Paul Kane's forward pass came over his shoulder. With half of the programme gone, they were in fifth position, and seemingly on course for a UEFA Cup place. St Mirren seemed to be their main challengers, with Hearts third bottom.

Hibs beat Hearts again at New Year, Eddie May scoring the only goal, to make it five points out of six, but then Weir needed a groin operation and he was lost to the side for the rest of the season. Still showing intent, however, Hibs paid Coventry £300,000 for their well-built centre, Keith Houchen, mostly remembered for his much televised cup final goal against Tottenham. They also had a bid of £275,000 for Michael O'Neill turned down by Newcastle United.

A comparatively kind series of cup draws involving Brechin, Motherwell and Alloa Athletic took Hibs to a semi-final against Celtic, but they were completely outplayed, especially on the right flank, where McIntyre was given too little help against Fulton. Celtic led 3–0 in 28 minutes, and Archibald's second-half goal was no more than a consolation.

So it remained in the league that Hibs best hopes of European football lay, and it did no harm to beat St Mirren 1–0 in the fifth last game. With three games to go, Hibs in fifth place were five points ahead of Hearts and St Mirren, and it seemed odds on their making it. Hibs took only one point from these three games, losing to Dundee United and then Celtic, and only drew the final one at home to Dundee because Findlay's speculative lob was held just over the line by the Dundee goalkeeper. Luckily, results elsewhere made this academic, as Hibs qualified by default when they lost to Dundee United.

Back in Europe

Alex Miller was still searching for the right blend, and, especially with European ties in prospect, there were still some funds available. He was busy before the start of the season—he bought Brian Hamilton from his former charges St Mirren for £275,000, and sold Eddie May for £165,000 to Brentford to help balance the books. Neale Cooper also came from St Mirren, at a bargain price of £40,000 to give more depth in defence. Miller also had to fine Andy Goram, now the club captain, for playing against Australia at cricket—Goram was still on Lancashire's books—and Steve Archibald for likewise ignoring instructions. Rangers made their customary early season jaunt to Easter Road, and lost for the third time of late, with Houchen and Weir scoring the two goals. Following the Hillsborough tragedy in England, there were new even tighter restrictions in force—for by no means the last time—and the crowd was restricted to 22,500. Tickets requested 'spectators to be seated at least fifteen minutes before kick-off'—even those for the main (standing) terracing!

The league cup run featured another extra-time defeat, this time at home at the hands of Dunfermline Athletic, and Hibs averaged a point a game in league matches through the autumn, so that the main focus was on the UEFA games against Videoton, and how to pronounce Szekesfehervar, where they came from. The first leg was at Easter Road, and while not on a par with the great European nights that fewer and fewer can remember, did provide drama, mainly because of the weakness of the Belgian referee, and the roughness of the tackling as the Hungarians kept Hibs to one goal. Graeme Mitchell was the unlikely scorer, with a looping header when the visiting goalkeeper was stranded after a strange effort to punch clear.

The return was more clear-cut, with West German officials. Mitchell was earmarked as a target early on, but still provided the cross for a definitive header by Houchen to put Hibs ahead in nine minutes and leaving Videoton to score three. Hibs retained possession in style, until around the hour mark, and in response to their fans who were somewhat restless about their team's lack of success, Videoton started some strongarm stuff again, lost a man sent off—Petras for a foul on Cooper—and a goal in quick succession. Houchen hit the post with a header, and Evans was first to the loose ball to score. Collins hit a marvellous third on the volley when Hamilton's thirty yarder came back off the bar, and Hibs were home and dry.

The second round against F.C. Liège, not to be confused with Standard Liège, also started at Easter Road, but was less successful. Chances were few in a typical tight tie, and Houchen missed the best one from the penalty spot. The second leg was also goalless. Given his experience, it was surprising that Archibald was omitted entirely, and when Houchen had to go off, Hibs did not have a replacement striker to go on. It proved costly. In extra time, the home captain de Sart, about to be harassed by Evans, swung at a Hibs' clearance about forty yards from goal, Goram seemed to see the danger late, and the ball crashed in off the crossbar behind him. In the second period of extra time, McGinlay had the ball in the net, but was ruled offside—television evidence later showed the decision to have been wrong—and Hibs were out.

Hibs were in contention again for a European place—albeit the last one again—and they had wins at Pittodrie on Boxing Day, to depose Aberdeen from the top, and Ibrox later in the season, but there was still the liklihood of dropping more points to the basement teams than their rivals, and in the end they lost out. They lost their third last game by the only goal at Motherwell, drew their penultimate one at home to Dundee, and also drew their last game at Dunfermline. With just a few minutes remaining at Dunfermline, Hibs were actually in fourth place in the league, but without even losing another goal, events elsewhere conspired to put them in seventh place at the close, on the same points as Celtic who were fifth.

John Collins might have had grounds for regretting his penalty miss in the draw against Dundee, but in fact he did get to Europe, because he was transferred to Celtic at the end of the season. It was the last of a further batch of comings and goings in the second half of the season. Ronnie Rosenthal of Standard Liège was nearly the first—he got as far as playing trials but the £500,000 asking price was an impediment—but Hibs did sign Mark McGraw from Morton, and, at the third attempt, Miller got Paul Wright, who had moved from Aberdeen to Queens Park Rangers. Wright's debut was exciting, coming on as a late substitute against Aberdeen. Hibs had led by 2–0 with only six minutes to go, but Aberdeen had drawn level courtesy of Van der Ark and a Hunter own goal, when Wright drove home an injury time winner. Injury time was not to prove too lucky for Wright in general, as he spent the latter part of the season out of action following the crude attentions of Hearts' Neil Berry in the final league derby of the season. On the departure side, Gordon Rae went to Partick Thistle for £65,000, and Peter Cormack, who had been Alex Miller's assistant since he had come to Easter Road, was stunned to be sacked by the manager just before the end of the season. By the time of Collins' transfer, the financial plight surrounding Hibs and their new parent company was beginning to come to light, and an entirely different episode in the club's history lay just round the corner.

— 11 —
FINANCIAL TIMES

S ince their inception, Hibs' had experienced the highs and lows of football—their world championship in 1887 and their successes of the 1950s being balanced by their inability to be accepted by the SFA, their going out of business in 1891 and nearly again around 1930. But the episode which started with David Duff's purchase of Kenny Waugh's controlling interest in Hibs in 1987 and led directly to the club facing extinction at the hands of Wallace Mercer in 1990 and again a year later when in receivership, was as traumatic as any. This chapter documents these troublesome times.

The Duff Takeover

It was in the summer of 1987 that Jim Gray, brother-in-law of David Duff, first sounded out Kenny Waugh about selling his interest in Hibs. Duff was born and brought up in Edinburgh and was educated at Trinity Academy where he played first XV rugby. His family had moved south, and Duff was now a lawyer, based in Swindon, with other interests in property, restaurants and a furniture business. He had been a Hibs' supporter from the age of five, and claimed to have watched Hibs during the previous season in the wing stand with Gray, pies and Bovril. It has, however, proved difficult to trace people who recall this scene of fraternal cosiness.

Waugh and Duff first met on the Isle of Man, where Hibs were competing in a pre-season competition. They watched Hibs fail to beat Stoke City, and get eliminated as a result. That was not a good omen. Duff next appeared in the Easter Road directors' box for the opening match in which Hibs beat Rangers.

Duff's offer was to buy the 500,000 Hibs' shares at £1.75, a total of £875,000. Waugh's share would be £710,000. In addition, Duff

The thousands who turned up at Easter Road to tell Wallace Mercer to keep his 'Hands off Hibs'

would take over the club's overdraft of about £300,000. Waugh would remain on the board, and two former Hibs' players would join it. So would Gray, who would be installed as managing director, as Duff would be in England most of the time. Waugh and his lawyers satisfied themselves that Duff was not fronting for someone else. In particular, David Rowland's name, of which more later, was not mentioned. Duff took control on August 24, in time to authorise the purchase of Neil Orr for £100,000 from West Ham. Orr made his debut against Queen of the South the next evening. Waugh and Gregor Cowan remained on the board. Duff promised 'a new tomorrow' and wanted Hibs 'to be the best run club in the country', as did we all.

Within a few days, there were further appointments to the board, but they were not those of former Hibs' players. Indeed the first was Sheila Rowland, who ran an all female lawyer's firm down south, and was more relevantly the wife of David Rowland. She became the first female director of a Scottish football club. Unlike her husband, Mrs Rowland proved a pleasant and popular member of the board, and despite a lot of pressure at times, always put Hibs ahead of personal interests. The second was Jeremy James, also London based, an accountant and a financial adviser of David Rowlands. Rowland was already well-known in financial circles for his involvement with Williams Hudson, the wharfing company behind his success as a whiz-kid in the sixties, and fall in the seventies. Williams Hudson had collapsed in 1982, and, as the BBC 'Focal Point' programme pointed out, had taken dozens of other companies down with it. It seems that Duff first met Rowland at a cocktail party, and it turned out that Rowland had loaned Duff £800,000 with which to make his bid for Hibs, so that the new chairman had only invested £99,000 of his own. James was effectively Rowland's nominee on the Hibs' board.

It was in an interview with John Gibson of the *Evening News* that the first inkling came of what was intended. The plan was to raise cash by selling shares to Hibs' supporters, the point, according to Duff, 'where sensible capitalist thinking met socialism', with the aim of building a stadium where sixteen or seventeen thousand came regularly and Easter Road was 'the shop window of an Edinburgh multi-business and the owners being the supporters themselves as shareholders'. He wanted posterity to view him and his brother-in-law as 'the men who underpinned Hibs and made them safe forever'. He also pointed out, in answer to the public concern that he was not at

This young Hibs' fan spoke for thousands

Easter Road only for some asset-stripping, that he could have invested his million pounds elsewhere; again that would seem to deny Rowland's influence over what he did.

The following July, 1988, Kenny Waugh was dismissed from the board, while in hospital for major surgery. This sparked off another chain of accusations, with a claim by Waugh for unpaid director's fees, and a 'very strong' but less specific counter-claim against him by the club.

The Flotation

By the start of the new season, Hibs had announced that they intended to float the company on the Unlisted Securities Market. The football club would be one of three subsidiaries of Edinburgh Hibernian plc. Two other subsidiaries, investing in property and leisure, would provide the funds with which Hibs would be able to compete with the Old Firm on equal terms. The shares issue would be pitched so that fans would be able to afford a stake in the club, but Duff would retain his majority holding.

The launch was on October 1, and it did not take commentators long to pick holes in it, Andrew Garfield for one was keeping a close eye on things for *The Scotsman*. Although there was no suggestion of anything illegal, the structure was 'very unusual'. The 7,300,000 shares were priced at 55p each, and at that price valued the company at just over £4,000,000.

Thirty per cent of the shares in Edinburgh Hibernian, or £1,200,000, were to go effectively to Rowland, in return for his 'expertise' in overseeing the takeover and share issue. The holding was partly in the name of a Panamanian company, Charcoal, which was owned by a Dutch registered company called Monaco, in turn owned by Rowland and his relatives. Duff received twenty per cent, worth £800,000 at the issue price, for his investment of £99,000.

With more blocks of shares in institutional hands, just under one third of the shares were left for the supporters, and the total amount raised was about £2,000,000. Of this sum, Rowland would get half of his loan repaid, with interest, making £500,000, which seemed to imply a fairly high rate of interest, and the costs of the flotation were about £400,000. That left little more than half. Less than a year later,

Hibs supporters show their defiance of Mercer in the rally at Easter Road

it was reported that Rowland's loan was more or less all repaid, so that of the sum raised, not much more than £500,000 was left for the stated grand designs of the club's new owners.

In addition, the arrangements meant that Duff could not be removed from the board without the agreement of Rowland, as the pair controlled a majority of the shares. That was normal inasmuch as most club chairmen control a majority of shares, but the implication to many fans was that they would have a hand in the running of the club. A number of independent chartered accountants asked by *The Scotsman* agreed that what the supporters had in fact done was to pay for Duff and Rowland to get 50% of the club for practically nothing. And Rowland had also the advantage of having his own nominee, Jeremy James, appointed to the Edinburgh Hibernian board.

Another important factor was that Duff and the Hibs' supporters had just over half of the shares under their control. That meant that if the leisure and pub activities were successful, then they could vote for the profits from them being channelled into the football club. If more than half of the shares had been in control of institutions, or individuals, who did not have the well-being of the football club at

The anti-Mercer rally at Easter Road

heart, the transfer of profits elsewhere to the loss-making football subsidiary would not have made sense. Usually in business, a chronically loss-making part of the business would be sold off if possible, and if that was not possible, it would be closed down. For the time being, that would not happen, but it would not take very many sales of supporters' shares to make it a possibility.

Nevertheless, the issue was judged a success, and the share price drifted upward and peaked at over 70p, and it was not long before the first investment was announced. The Talk of the Town in Exeter was bought for £1,000,000, with Duff estimating that the net income to Hibs would be £120,000 per annum. The purchase included a mortgage of £700,000 which seemed to confirm how much of the funds raised was actually available to invest. The Lenwood Sport And Country Club in north Devon was acquired a couple of months later.

The Rights Issue

Another major investment was announced in February 1988, that of Avon Inns, in a deal worth £5,750,000. This was to be financed by a

1:1 rights issue, that is, a further issue of of the same number of shares as was already in existence, with existing shareholders having first refusal on one new share for each one they already held. The price was to be above the flotation price of 55p, to raise another £4,000,000 but below the 71p at which the shares were then trading. It is common practice to pitch the price of rights issue shares below the current price, to induce shareholders to buy the new ones, because the price could be expected to settle somewhere in between the two levels.

The background was cloudy but worrying. Avon Inns was a portfolio of fifteen properties in the Bath area of south-west England. It was created out of the ashes of another company called Carrington Hotels, which had crashed owing more than £3,000,000 to the London and Suburban Land and Building Company. And Jeremy James was a director of LSLB when they called in the receivers. Avon Inns had been bought from the receiver by a company called Inoco. It so happened that, since the Williams Hudson failure in 1982, Inoco was Rowland's first essay into a quoted company, although it lost its stock exchange listing soon afterwards when it switched its attention from oil to property. Rowland had also recently paid over $40 million for a controlling interest in Gulf Resources and Chemical Corporation, an American oil company worth about $180m. The Avon chain of restaurants and pubs were apparently surplus to requirements, as Inoco's 'only leisure interests' and were not consistent with Inoco's development programme, and so Rowland was kind enough to let them go 'virtually at cost' to Hibernian Leisure. Had that been true, it would seem to have begged the question of why Inoco bought Avon Inns in the first place. There was also the question of why, unusually, the price was based more on property values, which were still high after the boom of the late eighties, than turnover. Duff claimed that the chain would bring Hibs in about £800,000 in the first year— instead it lost twice as much. It also transpired that Exeter's Talk of the Town, and the Lenwood Sport and Country Club in Devon had both been bought from receivers called in by James' company.

The rights issue took place in the autumn, a year after the flotation, and the price was 55p again. This time it was not a success. Only 220 of the 1475 shareholders bought just two per cent of the new shares. The share of the club owned by David Duff and the Hibs' supporters was therefore diluted from approximately one half to one quarter. The

Joe Baker kisses the Easter Road turf during the anti-Mercer rally

new shares were 'placed' with institutions, and Inoco received a large block to make up the balance of the purchase price. Rowland had previously sold his personal holding, 15% of the company, for at least £1,500,000, which was all profit as he had been given these shares for nothing. Now through Inoco, his holding was effectively 30% again. Most of the institutions were based overseas, and they would presumably hold them on a less sympathetic basis than the Hibs' fans. The balance of power had therefore moved from Duff and the supporters into unfriendly hands, and disaster beckoned.

The Mercer Affair

At Easter Road, Duff was under considerable pressure from both the Rowland camp and the bank to provide some deal or transfer a player, or initiate a bid for the club, before the end of the financial year in July. From an issue price of 55p, and a peak of about 72p, the shares had traded as low as 17p, and were currently hovering around the 20p mark, and in May *Scotland on Sunday* forecast troubles ahead in the boardroom. Allan Munro, a well respected Edinburgh fund manager, had been brought on to the board at the start of the year, but threatened to resign because of lack of financial and other controls.

Avon Inns had been a disaster, and Duff, seemed to be willing to consider an offer either for his interest, or for the whole company. The half-year figures brought the total losses to date to about £2,000,000 and the debt to at least £4,500,000, compared to the overdraft of £300,000 which Duff had inherited.

As early as February 1990, there were moves afoot which were to lead to the threatened disaster scenario. Ronnie McNeill, who had financial interests in both Edinburgh and London, discovered that Rowland's shares could be available, and he made the contact with Hibs' supporters in Edinburgh who might join him in buying into the club, and thereby get a majority of the shares once again into friendly hands. An Edinburgh stockbroker, David Low, became involved. Wallace Mercer was approached about a friendly merger with Hearts. The combined club would play at a new super stadium at Hermiston, but that is another story. From this developed the hostile bid which Mercer launched in early June, with the help of Rowland, and having dropped McNeill and the other original participants, who were quite opposed to Mercer's aims.

A Hibs' board meeting was arranged by Rowland for Sunday June 3rd, in Inoco's offices in London. The Hibs' directors present were

Margo MacDonald chaired the 'Hands off Hibs' rally at the Usher Hall

Kenny McLean addresses the audience at the Usher Hall

Duff, Gray and Munro, and it had been suggested to them that a bid might be in the offing from a source which might not be welcome. At a meeting in Edinburgh, the three speculated about who it could be—Robert Maxwell's name was one discussed. Once at Inoco late on that Sunday afternoon, Duff was summoned to the inner sanctum, to emerge shell-shocked an hour or so later. It was not Maxwell but Wallace Mercer who had been introduced as the prospective buyer. A lengthy discussion followed. Mercer explained at length his 'vision' of one Edinburgh club able to compete with the Old Firm and everybody else in Europe. Unfortunately that had to mean the end of Hibs and the closure of Easter Road, but that was just the price of progress. Duff, Gray and Munro were astonished. Mercer was bidding 40p per share, nearly double the market price. He could already count on Rowland's block of shares, and at that price had every right to expect his offer to be accepted by most of the institutions as well. In buoyant mood, he seemed to consider the takeover as a *fait accompli*, and seemed surprised that Duff had declined his cheque for his shares. Then the Hibs' men were invited to dinner, and the whole party adjourned to the Hilton, where McNeill was a guest, and where Mercer was full of himself and picked up the bill. Most of Mercer's attention was focussed on Munro, almost to the point of ignoring his other guests. He seemed to believe that Duff had agreed to appear at the Caledonian Hotel the following morning to help Mercer present the deal as an agreed merger. Duff however did not commit his 12% or so of the shares for the tempting £700,000 on offer, together with the vice-chairmanship of the new company, but it was only later, when the Scottish party discussed the situation in Duff's London flat, that he was dissuaded from being on Mercer's platform in the morning, and Mercer was appraised of the change of plan as they all prepared to board the early shuttle north.

It was the following morning, Monday June 4th, that the story broke on the morning radio headlines. The city was told that Hibs had played their last game at Easter Road, that the ground would be closed and that the capital's football would in future be concentrated in a super Hearts club.

The welter of emotions, confusion, anger and dismay, among Hibs supporters, particularly the many who laid siege to Easter Road clamouring for news and reassurance, was widely reported. Duff could only say that no offer document had been received, and until it had, he could make no comment, but at a further Edinburgh Hibernian board meeting in London, the bid was voted down by four to two, with Sheila Rowland voting against her husband. There was less reporting of the hundreds who vented their anger in the vicinity of Mercer's house. That was discouraged for the sake of public order.

There was also much uninformed speculation about the consequences, and in particular, about the team which the new Hearts would be able to field. The question arose for example of whether Andy Goram or Henry Smith would be the number one goalkeeper. Quite apart from there being no doubt which one any manager would prefer, the whole line of discussion overlooked the fact that if Hibs had to withdraw from the league, the players' contracts would revert to the league, not to Hearts, unless it was an agreed merger which of course by this time it was clearly not.

The legal position seemed quite clear. If Mercer could garner more than fifty per cent of the shares, then he had control of the holding company Edinburgh Hibernian and therefore the football club. There were still hurdles for him to overcome, however, or, from the other point of view, areas of defence still open to the pro-Hibs faction. These included the rules of the Scottish League, Company rules regarding takeovers, the Office of Fair Trading and, not to be underestimated, the force of public opinion. There was also the proviso in the offer that it lapsed if the case was referred to the Monopolies and Mergers Commission.

Mercer kept his cards pretty close to the microphone, and received a disproportionate amount of coverage on all sorts of things, and so the Hibs lobby had to make sure that their point was got across as well, and also to co-ordinate the efforts of those sympathetic to their cause into a focussed and efficient response. David Duff was certainly not the man for this, widely being held to blame for the whole business, and for collusion in it by many, but a meeting of a large group at the Hibs' Supporters' club ended with the creation of the 'Hands Off Hibs' campaign, led by ex-vice chairman Kenny McLean. The first major event was a rally at Easter Road on June 9th and a trust fund was set up to buy shares to fight off Mercer. At an early date Allan Munro enlisted the support of Tom Farmer, Kwik-Fit boss, who, while not a football fan himself, was proud of his Leith background and his family's role in the in the club's history. Other principle projects of the movement were the handing in to No. 10 Downing Street a petition of fifty thousand names, and a rally at the Usher Hall, chaired by Margo MacDonald on July 2nd. Among the platform guests, apart from Messrs. Duff and Gray were Tom Farmer and John Robertson of Hearts.

There was an enormous amount of support for Hibs, from MPs, Lothian Regional Council, Edinburgh District Council, the Scottish Professional Footballers Association, the STUC amongst many others. An *Evening News* survey found that Hearts supporters were strongly against Mercer's bid, never mind those of Hibs. And while Hibs had been discussed in the United Nations during their tour to Nigeria in 1967, and the House of Commons in the seventies, this time they reached new heights with John Leslie bringing the issue up on BBC TV's 'Blue Peter' programme.

From the football authorities' point of view, a merger of the two clubs, if that was how it was to be presented, would require league approval. Following concerns over dealings in England, a new rule had been drafted that the Management Committee should 'have regard to the interest and public profile of Association Football, its players, spectators and others concerned with the game' In any case, in order to get that far, Mercer would be in breach of the league rules which limited any person's beneficial holding to shares in one club. What was not clear was whether he could he get round that by having his Hibs' shares in, for example, his wife's name.

On company law, the relevant part was that Mercer required more than 75% of the shares to pass an extraordinary resolution within Edinburgh Hibernian. Without this majority, it was not clear why the Edinburgh Hibernian board could not use its 100% holding to instruct the Hibernian FC board to disband the club, but in any case, starving it of investment and income would soon amount to the same thing. It was not clear what Mercer would do in this situation, but it was soon evident that it would be the outcome. With Mercer's bid of 40p, the share price rose to the 35–40p range, and Tom Farmer was able to buy a block of just over 5% of the shares. When this was added to the holdings of David Duff and the supporters, the sum was nearly one-third of the total. It may have been that the first target of more than 25% had been met without Farmer's shares, but in either case, Duff's holding seemed vital. What did not seem to be generally known at this time was that the Bank of Scotland's financing of Mercer's bid was dependant on his winning more than 75% of the shares. Since Edinburgh Hibernian's major shareholder Rowland had pledged his shares and could probably for others, the Bank of Scotland had probably been given cause to believe that the merger would be an agreed one, and might have been less happy about being involved in such a sensitive area between two of its higher profile customers otherwise.

The thought occurred to some that since Mercer had more than 75% of Hearts' shares, the simplest thing would be to close down Hearts and focus his constructive attention to Hibs, but somehow that did not seem likely.

From the OFT point of view, they were asked by Hibs to consider the proposed situation with regard to a possible referral to the Monopolies and Mergers Commission. The OFT considered whether Hearts and Hibs together provided more than 25% of professional football entertainment in Edinburgh. Hearts had argued that the market should have been Scotland rather than Edinburgh, but the OFT ruled for Hibs that the case fell within the guidelines for referral to the MMC. Mercer's bid may well have failed on these grounds, but it was withdrawn before this procedure went any further.

All this was before the offer document was even available. The offer was to close on July 2nd, about four weeks after the bid was launched. The document added little to the speculation that was relevant. While it quite appropriately highlighted the poor running of Edinburgh Hibernian, it failed to give much comfort about Hearts' own financial strength. Hearts valued Edinburgh Hibernian at 23.7p per share to show that their offer was generous.

Hibs replied with a value at 50.3p to show it was not. Apart from admitting that their debts were approaching £6m, that players would have to be sold and that the present management had got things badly wrong, the Hibs' document said nothing either. The Hearts valuation meant the whole company was valued at £3.62m, which they started using as a get-out because the assets were presented as being below the minimum Hearts wanted to go ahead. By now, one could sense that Mercer's resolve was weakening, and he started talking about Hibs' debts being so high it would not be worth taking them over. There was also the realisation, as Tom Farmer's friend Tom Harrison bought another block of shares, that the 75% was pie in the sky.

While there was little doubt about Hibs' problems, an independent survey by Price Waterhouse showed that if surplusses from revaluing grounds were excluded—just over half the clubs covered did this to strengthen their balance sheets—then three clubs, Hibs, Dunfermline and Hearts, would have deficits on their balance sheets. Moreover, Hearts present banking facilities had only been granted on the basis that Mercer remained as chief executive with his company, Pentland Securities, the main shareholder.

The claims and counter-claims went on, until the votes were counted. Mercer had 62.76% of them—more than most people expected—and extended the offer for a week. Usually in the case where a takeover bid wins more than half the shares, the chairman of the outbid company accepts the bid for his own shares and advises others to do the same. David Duff did not follow that line which would have set up Mercer within one per cent of target even if nobody followed the advice. Publicly, Hibs took comfort that, Rowland apart, more than half the votes were cast for Hibs.

In a separate development, Kenny Waugh stepped in to take a further block which became available, believed to have come from the GRE. The other British instutions involved had already sold to Farmer and Harrison. The other institutions were overseas, and difficult to identify, as Hibs found when they had to get a court interdict for them to identify the beneficial owners so they could be contacted. Mercer tried a new tack by offering Hibs the chance to remain independent, to play at Easter Road for another season before joining Hearts at the new stadium at Hermiston, and be sold off from the holding company. This seemed to confirm that the Hermiston project and its financing was at the heart of the whole matter.

Hibs refused, and so little changed during the extra week. Duff was under intense pressure to sell his holding, and was even said to have received an offer of £1 per share by telephone in the Edinburgh Hibernian advisers' offices at lunchtime the following Friday, a few hours before Mercer withdrew his bid.

It was not long before Rowland, apparently 'astonished' that Duff had refused to negotiate with Mercer during the extra week, and on the grounds that he had not advised shareholders correctly, initiated an action to sue Duff and his fellow directors for the £1,500,000 he would have made had his scheme with Mercer succeeded, (over and above the earlier £1,500,000 and the high interest on his original loan of course).

The Climbdown

There had been signs towards the end of the campaign that Mercer was cooling off, and when there was no appreciable difference in his position during the extra week, that is, Duff did not change his mind and sell out, it was not a great surprise when he pulled out. Usually in a takeover attempt, a majority such as Mercer had achieved is easily enough to succeed in most aims of the taker-over, so what factors influenced Mercer's decision to quit?

Firstly, there was the condition on Mercer's getting the funding he required that he get commitments in respect of more than 75% of the shares. Mercer later claimed that he had been given the go ahead with only 50%, but in any case the bank may not have been entirely happy with how things had developed since Mercer first approached them.

Secondly, Mercer claimed to have won the financial argument but lost the social one. By the financial argument, he seemed to mean that he had achieved a majority of shares. What this amounted to was the offer to buy the shares of a debt-ridden company which went to the wall within a year anyway, with the object of closing down its only profitable subsidiary, the football club, was accepted by some of the shareholders. The football club of course was of value mainly as a going concern, as was shown a year later. Moreover, he was going to pay almost twice the going rate for shares, quite apart from any late offer to Duff. Mercer's talk towards the end of the campaign, about Hibs assets being lower than expected, and their debts higher, seemed to be a belated recognition that he had got his sums wrong. The quotes we do not have reflect what the minority shareholders of Hearts thought of this coup. Mercer was quoted later saying convincingly: 'I want people to believe me when I say I was not trying to destroy Hibs'.

Thirdly, the social argument finally seemed to get through to him. Mercer said that 'there is no point in going ahead with a merger if one party is implacably opposed to it'. This was towards the end of the campaign. It was a pity that that brainwave had not occurred a month earlier.If he had understood football fans, it would have. If he had gone ahead, his own life would not have been worth living in Edinburgh, the only natural stage for the chairman of the capital's only top club, and may well have been in danger. By September, when Mercer sacked Hearts' most successful manager for years and had to pay out compensation to get a new one, he had achieved the almost impossible, for one who was neither Jimmy Hill nor a member of the Old Firm, by being so heartily disliked by both sides of Edinburgh's football community.

As it was, the pressure was telling. Mercer later said 'My wife, son and daughter have been under constant pressure over the past six weeks—with threats, phone calls and so on. The police told me not to mention it because it increases the tension'. That was to the *Sunday Mail*.

Fourthly, Mercer's super stadium project at Hermiston seemed to be central to his vision for the capital's football and its followers, and that was rapidly running into the sand. Mercer had said 'I suppose I would truthfully have to describe myself as a controlled egomaniac' in the infamous tome 'Heart to Heart'. Apart from being a contradiction in terms, you may consider whether egomania is a trait you would want or expect in one whose only aim was shaping a better future for your club.

Fifthly, the OFT had ruled in Hibs' favour that a monopolistic situation would arise in Edinburgh football, and accepted that the case came into the guidelines for referral to the Monopolies and Mergers Commission. Hearts had argued that the appropriate 'market' was Scotland rather than Edinburgh and lost. Mercer's aims may have foundered on this alone.

The Receivership

If there was any upside from Mercer's involvement with Hibs, it was that he exposed the perilous financial state of the club, or at least its parent company. Help was at hand, though, and the board was reshaped by Farmer and Munro. Alister Dow, a chartered accountant with a sound reputation in the Scottish business community, was brought in as chairman of the plc, with Duff giving up the position but remaining on the board. Tom Farmer and Tom Harrison both joined the board. Rowland remained on it, and was joined by another nominee, Derek Moran. Moran at least turned out to constructive and helpful, albeit within the restrictive brief from Rowland. Duff also vacated the chair of the football club, with Gray taking over his responsibilities.

To dismiss the developments of the following months in a paragraph does scant justice to the efforts of Farmer and the others to find an acceptable solution which kept the football club alive, but ultimately it boiled down to an incompatibilty of interests. The plans were mostly variations of a theme to split the football club from its parent, either playing at Easter Road for a while, but probably having to move out at some time, probably to Meadowbank, and sell Easter Road. The pro-Hibs directors together with the Bank of Scotland were intent on restructuring the Company into three separate operating divisions, a football club, a property division and a leisure division. The likelihood was that the football club could stay at Easter Road for a while but would have to move out at some time and sell the ground. In the other corner was Rowland, for practical purposes in comtrol of the sixty per cent or so of shares which had been committed to Mercer, and demanding another pound of flesh. The bank had kept the door open mainly because it had belief in Farmer, Harrison and Munro, but ultimately a VAT bill went unpaid and the receivers were called in. That was quite a long paragraph so maybe it should have been two.

The receivers were called in to Edinburgh Hibernian, or Forth Investments as it had renamed itself. The football club continued to run under chief executive Jim Gray, and the receivers hoped to sell it off separately. There were two bids. Former charman, Kenny Waugh, put together an offer, which would have seen him back as chairman. Tom Farmer led and financed a consortium which included the leaders of the Hands Off Hibs campaign, which the receivers chose as the 'preferred bidder'. This is a method by which the receivers enter into serious talks with only one bidder, but the deal is not tied up at that stage until the details are agreed. In due course they were. The consortium bought the football club and the Easter Road ground in separate deals, so that Tom Farmer effectively owns both, but as separate entities. The new board consisted initially of Douglas Cromb, the new chairman, Kenny McLean, Tom O'Malley and Allan Munro, with Tom Farmer taking a back seat, but eventually to install Robert Huthersall as his representative. Their first act was to go to Easter Road and dismiss Gray along with commercial manager Raymond Sparkes.

— 12 —
FARMER'S DEN

At the start of every season there is something special about seeing your team run out for the first time, but for Hibs' supporters after the trauma of the summer the start of season 1990–91 meant more. Hibs did not play at Easter Road until September 1st., against Rangers, after no fewer than nine friendly and competitive matches elsewhere. They had beaten teams like Cowdenbeath and the Prussians of Hameln, whose footballers have never threatened the Pied Piper among the local attractions but defeats included one at Magdeburg, a depressing town in what had been East Germany, and, worse, a league cup exit at Starks Park, Kirkcaldy.

By now it was common knowledge that Hibs were in dire financial straits, and there was no money for players, despite the sum 'in the region of £1 million' which Celtic paid for John Collins. There were other problems. Paul Kane was out of contract, and determined to leave. Andy Goram missed training and the plane to Germany, apparently because a proposed move back to Oldham had not come off. Paul Wright was back after the incident with Berry, but Brian Hamilton's leg-break would need more time.

There was also the manager's position, which was under threat from a faction on the board. This group wanted David Hay to come, and even made contact while Hibs were in England. There was no agreement for that move however, and Miller not only stayed but extended his contract for another two years. He must have wondered why when almost at once he had to take his team to Pittodrie minus seven players. In addition, there were rumours that Michael Knighton, who had tried and failed to take over Manchester United, might bid for Hibs.

Hibs drew with Rangers in that first home match, and a fortnight later came the predictable flash point with Hearts' visit. Mercer made a lot of noise about being the first off the bus, but eventually bowed to police advice to stay away. This frustrated a plan by the Hibs' casuals to attack him in the stand, but it did not stop all the trouble. Mercer had just sacked Hearts' most successful manager for years for not winning anything, so that he was not exactly flavour of the month with their fans either. Andy Goram and John Robertson had to separate fighting fans just after Hearts' opening goal in thirteen minutes, and the game was held up for ten minutes. That did not break the flow of play, because there wasn't any. Hearts were three up at half-time and finished the same way. Mercer later said the trouble was his fault, and for once he was right. It was a good day to get over with.

It was vital for Hibs to avoid relegation because of their financial position, and there were some things in their favour. Firstly, St Mirren and Dunfermline were in the Premier Division, so it would not take world beaters to stay up. After seven games, Hibs had six points, two ahead of that pair. Secondly, Andy Goram signed a three year contract, and most of the points Hibs won seemed to have been earned by the goalkeeper. And thirdly, Murdo Macleod came to Hibs from Borussia Dortmund to be player/assistant manager. Dunfermline wanted him too, but it was the offer of the managerial position that swung Macleod's choice Hibs' way. His debut was not overly auspicious— Willie Miller volleyed a completely unnecessary last minute own goal at Tannadice to give Dundee United a 1–0 win.

Meanwhile, the league struggle went on. Hibs were hammered 4–0 at Ibrox, but were sixth, if only two points above Hearts who were bottom. Another unpleasant derby at Tynecastle, score 1–1, was followed by a home defeat by Celtic, and Hibs were only one point off the bottom. A draw with Dundee United made the margin over St Mirren two points again, but then Hibs lost by the only goal at Paisley, to a team that finished with nine men. Then came another horrific New Year derby.

Around this time, even when Hibs played well against Hearts, the fates conspired to make sure they did not win. This was such an occasion. By half-time, Hearts were three up. Tosh McKinlay tries a shot-cum-something from near half-way, and Willie Miller, in the flight path close to the penalty spot, dummied it past Goram. For the third goal, Goram came out of his box to head clear, and headed straight to Gary Mackay, who scored easily. Despite a draw at Celtic

Park, Hibs were now a point adrift, and they lost their next games to Aberdeen and Rangers.

There was not much going right, but Falkirk came to Hibs' aid by getting a proposal to extend the Premier Division to twelve clubs, with no relegation that year, passed, despite Rangers, Celtic, Hearts, Aberdeen and Dundee United opposing it. Effectively it saved Hibs from relegation and the consequences that might have brought. The final game was between St Mirren and Hibs at Paisley. Not many were there to see it. Hibs lost 1–0, and finished second bottom, two points behind Dunfermline.

The Skol Cup

Paul Wright had finished Hibs' top scorer—with six goals—and he forecast that Hibs would win a European place the following season, which Hibs did by the shortest route—winning the Skol League Cup. But any future career as a seer was jeopardised by Wright's omitting to mention that he would be playing for St Johnstone by then. That transfer took place during the pre-season matches, and Paul was replaced by his namesake Keith, bought from Dundee for £420,000, the following day. Keith Houchen went to Port Vale for £100,000. A major loss was that of Andy Goram, who joined Rangers for £1m as part of the deal with Hibs' rescue from receivership. John Burridge, thirty-nine years old and a man of many clubs, took over, apparently until one or other of Hibs' three outstanding young keepers, Reid, Gardiner or Woods, was ready.

Hibs beat Stirling easily in the first tie, but then survived a cliff-hanger at Kilmarnock. Murdo Macleod equalised Kilmarnock's first goal when their second looked more likely, and it took a Pat McGinlay goal two minutes after Kilmarnock had made it 2–2 to squeeze Hibs through. In the non-seeded quarter-final draw, a tie with Ayr was a good draw, and Hibs won 2–0 at Somerset Park. That took them to the semi-finals, and Hibs drew Rangers at Hampden.

If anything personified the rebirth of Hibs then it was this performance, and half-way through the first half they scored. Andy Goram came out to meet a cross at the edge of the penalty area, and seemed to alter his run, not for the first time, to make sure that he made good contact with an opponent as well as the ball. The goalkeeper had a

Murdo Macleod holds the Skol Cup aloft

weight advantage over most opposing forwards. This time it was Mark
McGraw who was clattered to the ground, but the goalkeeper got his
due desserts. His punched clearance only reached Mickey Weir on the
Hibs' right, and Goram was still stranded when the winger measured
a cross for Keith Wright to head home. With two Rangers' defenders
apparently guarding the goalline, there was no question of offside.
Hibs had one scare in the second half when a free-kick hit their post
and Burridge did well to foil McCoist from the rebound, but they were
well worth their win on the night.

The same could not be said of Dunfermline, who remained in their
tie with Airdrie only because they were awarded a late penalty when
the Airdrie captain Sandison was outside the area and did not handle
the ball. But all's fair etc. etc. and it was Dunfermline that Hibs met
in the final.

The most striking feature of the final was the size of the Hibs'
support, at least three quarters of the attendance that was however
limited to about forty thousand because of the organisational inability
and intransigence of the authorities and the police. The gates were
closed with many more Hibs' fans outside. The game itself was very

low key. The main incident in the first half was an injury to goalkeeper Rhodes when Wright lost his footing going with the goalkeeper for a long ball. After the interval, Hibs stepped up the pace, and in four minutes they scored; Weir was brought down and Tommy McIntyre coolly converted the penalty. There was always some danger with such a slender lead, even if the Dunfermline raids seemed occasional and anaemic, but the game was sealed in the closing phase when Wright was sent through and slipped the ball past Rhodes for the second goal. It meant that the striker had scored in every round.

It had been a job professionally if unexcitingly done, and Murdo Macleod was presented with the trophy. It was paraded through Edinburgh and then acclaimed at Easter Road. Or so I heard on the car radio while crawling home along the M8 with everybody else.

Hibs had also been doing comparatively well in the league. The improvement came from the first game when Weir and Pat McGinlay each scored twice in a one-sided 4–1 win against St. Mirren. Hibs colours were not lowered until the final game in the first quarter, at Ibrox, and even then it took an own goal by Tortolano to put Rangers in the lead for the first time after an hour, and two goals in the last ten minutes to give Rangers a 4–2 win. But a lot of the games were drawn, and Hibs were not yet serious contenders. Their New Year draw with Hearts was their third of the season, but the defeat by Rangers that followed was also their third of the season and enabled the Ibrox side

Keith Wright is welcomed to Easter Road by Hibs' Directors

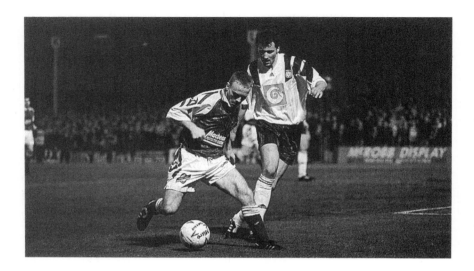

Mickey Weir closely marked by an Anderlecht defender

to leapfrog Hearts at the top. Rangers' fourth win over Hibs put them seven points clear. Hibs slipped to fifth, perhaps no surprise when they had a European place already secured, and in their final match won at Parkhead, to deny Celtic the other UEFA spot in favour of Hearts.

Anderlecht

Hibs' reward for winning the Skol Cup was a tilt at Anderlecht's expensive and talented team, with the second leg in the southern suburb of Brussels where their opponents had won three European trophies in the past twenty years or so. Anderlecht's squad included Jean Paul de Sart, whom Hibs remembered from F.C. Liege, and before they met Hibs they gave a demonstration of what maybe lay in store by winning 6–1 away to the said F.C.Liege.

Hibs' form before the UEFA tie was average, even with the addition of Darren Jackson from Dundee United to the squad. They had another tense league cup-tie at Kilmarnock but lost to two early goals in extra time. They had a as difficult start to the league as was then possible, but their 3–0 defeat at Aberdeen was followed by a win at Motherwell and a draw at home with Rangers. Off the field, the £400,000 they had to pay for Jackson was less than half United's inflated demand,

The Hibs team of 1992–93

and elsewhere, Hibs, along with St Johnstone, joined the group of clubs which intended to break away from the league because of the forty-four game programme the twelve team format implied. There was some irony in that, since Hibs of course had voted for the new structure when their own survival was in doubt, and if they had not, the proposal would not have been passed.

The first leg game against Anderlecht brought some reminiscence of the big European nights of twenty years and more earlier, although new UEFA regulations brought the ground's capacity to another low, about fifteen thousand. And Hibs got off to the best possible start; Jackson's shot was not held by the goalkeeper, and Dave Beaumont was on hand to score his first goal for Hibs from four yards. Anderlecht then started to play the ball ominously around, and near the interval Versavel, a first class attacking midfielder, got into the Hibs' penalty area only for Burridge to bring him down. Degryse scored from the spot.

The second half was a continuation of the first. Anderlecht played confidently and leisurely, giving the impression that a draw would suit them. Then Degryse passed forward between Beaumont and Orr, the defence was caught out, and van Vossen lobbed Burridge to put the Belgians ahead. It was in the remaining twenty-odd minutes that the game exploded. Weir was sent off for a petulant but harmless foul that had his opponent writhing on the ground; shortly afterwards, the same person, taking a throw-in, was hit by some coins and the German referee, who did not seem to be in full control, threatened to take the teams off if it didn't stop. Hibs were now playing more with heart than skill, but it paid off. Wright hit the underside of the bar, and then McGinlay clipped a pass into the far corner to give Hibs a draw and Anderlecht some anxious moments before the final whistle. But it would still take an outstanding performance to win the tie.

The return in the Constant van der Stock Stadium was two weeks later, and this time Hibs got off to the worst possible start. Tortolano was lucky not to be ordered off for a tackle in the opening seconds, and in only five minutes, Burridge seemed slow down to a soft shot from Nills which went in at his right-hand post. The Hibs' defence seemed to be standing off their opponents too much, there were some nervy performances and their hesitance nearly resulted in van Vossen scoring a second. Instead, Tortolano swung the ball over from Hibs' left, Hamilton returned it square across the goal and Jackson scored from eight yards. But Anderlecht continued to dominate, and the Hibs' strikers were left with little support. The same pattern continued most

Darren Jackson, Mickey Weir and Kevin McAllister before a friendly at Stirling

Steven Tweed, Pat McGinlay and Willie Miller

of the second half, but in a rare excursion, the ball was played in from the left, and Jackson glanced it past the goalkeeper. The only time the Hibs' support stopped singing all game was the agonised pause until the ball bounced just wide. The final minutes were the most exciting, with Hibs introducing Evans and making every effort to score once more, but it was not to be, and Anderlecht went through.

The Anderlecht tie was easily the highlight of the season, despite Hibs reaching the semi-finals of the Scottish Cup. To do that they beat St Mirren and St Johnstone, and in between were more than a little fortunate to draw at Cowdenbeath, before scraping through by the only goal in the replay. The semi-final at Tynecastle against Aberdeen was a dreadful game, made worse by the Dons scoring the only goal. Hibs finished the season in an undistinguished midfield position, at which point Murdo Macleod left the club; Alex Miller offerred Macleod a contract which reflected that he would in future be assistant manager but not a player, and Macleod would not agree to that.

There were more changes in personnel for 1993–94. The major signing seemed to be Falkirk's winger Kevin McAllister, for £235,000, especially as Mickey Weir was out of contract and out of sorts. With less aplomb and on a free transfer, Alex Miller also brought Jim Leighton to Easter Road. Leighton had been Scotland's goalkeeper until 1990, when his confidence and career took a nose-dive following the FA Cup Final between Manchester United and Crystal Palace, to the point where he had been signed from Dundee reserves.

Pat McGinlay had joined Celtic, so a tribunal had to sort out the respective valuations of £245,000 and £900,000, and Graeme Mitchell missed the start following stomach surgery. The fee was later fixed at £525,000, and part of it went to buy Michael O'Neill, Dundee United's gifted Irishman who had turned Hibs down on a pervious occasion. Even with McAllister and Leighton, Hibs' prospects were put as 'no better than top half of the table', and a goalless draw against Partick Thistle seemed to stress the point.

Optimism was in larger measure shortly afterwards, however, as Hibs produced some good form in both the league and league cup. In the latter, Alloa and Dundee were disposed of as one would expect, and then came a harder test against Partick Thistle, one of the sides using Firhill. Leighton had taken over as Hibs' number one keeper, but he blotted his copybook by coming for as long ball and being outjumped by Grant who headed home. McAllister equalised and scored Hibs second goal, as the game, a thriller beyond all reasonable hopes based on previous encounters, went into a penalty shoot-out. It was then that Leighton really paid his way, with three saves to take Hibs through to a semi-final with Dundee United. This was at Tynecastle, despite complaints by Jim Maclean's side about the venue.

The semi-final was a tense affair. The only goal came in ten minutes, and was superb. McAllister picked up a loose ball near halfway, and skipped through going left, when Darren Jackson came in at an angle to send an unsaveable grounder into the corner of the net. Hibs had to soak up a lot of pressure for the rest of the game, and Leighton was in fine fettle again, but in truth the few chances which Hibs were able to create were the clearer, and they might well have won by a bigger margin.

The final was at Parkhead, and against Rangers. Hibs competed well, but were always struggling against the collar, and when during the second half, an interchange between Hateley and Durrant ended with the latter lobbing Leighton, the issue seemed settled. But within a couple of minutes, Keith Wright took the ball wide left in the Rangers' penalty area, and his fierce cross went into the net off McPherson for the equaliser. Hibs then had their best spell, and came close to scoring, especially McAllister, whose deliberate drive from an angle shaved the post. Then McCoist came on, and with eight minutes to go, his lucky overhead attempt found Leighton just too far out, and this time Hibs could not come back.

But Hibs had also improved from their first league game, and when the won 2–0 at Motherwell to finish the first quarter, they were two points clear at the top; their only defeat had been against Rangers, but that changed again when Hearts came to Easter Road on October 30th. The Tynecastle side had fallen from grace so that they were usually to be found in the division's lower reaches, and indeed the two goals they scored to win this game were their first away goals of the season. By the time that Hibs drew 0–0 with St Johnstone in December, they had won only one from ten, but thereafter their 1–0 defeat at Parkhead was their only defeat in ten. With the number of games now being drawn in the Premier Division, these statistics sound more dramatic than they were. What was dramatic was how their season suddenly ended.

In the league, it was a visit to Ibrox which caused the trouble—not the fact that they lost, but the manner of it. In the first half, not only did referee McCluskey fail to act when Evans was floored by Robertson in the home penalty area, but both he and his linesman seemed to see nothing wrong with Durie's manhandling of Farrell prior to his scoring from Hateley's pass. Feelings rose, and there was a welter of bookings. Willie Miller was lucky not to be sent off, and Gordon Hunter unlucky that he was, under the 'last man' rule which led to the second goal.

The famous Golden Gagoules as modelled by Falkirk fans

Hibs fans watch the Stenhousemuir Scottish cup-tie on giant screens at Murrayfield Ice Rink

Hibs' cup exit was at the hands of Hearts, and of the many derbies during the depressing series of non-wins that Hibs should have won, was the most so. Robertson scored in two minutes and for the next eighty-six, Hearts had to play second fiddle. In the five minutes before half-time, Keith Wright equalised, McAllister hit the post, and Levein was inches away from a panicky own goal. The second half brought more Hibs pressure, but no goals until with four minutes to go, a long ball to Foster caught the Hibs' defence a bit flat-footed, and Hearts' arch-striker ran through, without ever having the ball under control, to hit it under Leighton with his shin for his first goal in two seasons.

From this what in political speak is now known as a double whammy, Hibs season disintegrated, even although in theory their European chances were still quite bright. A total of nine goals in the last fifteen league games ensured that they didn't stay that way, and the season petered out. Hibs lost 4–0 at Dens Park in the second last game, and finished with a 0–0 draw with Kilmarnock, with the sponsors' 'man of the match' award going to Brian Hamilton who had arguably his worst game since joining the club.

It was much the same team which started the new season more

Gordon Hunter celebrates his winner at Tynecastle

drastically; the only change was Tommy McIntyre's departure to Airdrie, although Keith Wright missed the first half of the season through injury. There was a perception that Hibs had now consolidated their position above the relegation group, and were ready to move a step further than of late. Still, it was a shock when Hibs posted the day's biggest win against Dundee United, now managed by Ivan Golac, a friendlier Serb than most of his compatriots seem to be. It was unreal to watch United, usually so boringly effective in defence, in total disarray in a second half which also marked the first goal for Kevin Harper, whose early displays earned comparisons with the teenage Joe Baker. Golac fined both himself and his players, but few realised what sort of season that game was to start for the Tannadice side.

Apart from the marked difference in their relationship with Dundee United that that result was to herald, Hibs also ended their poor sequence against Hearts; the only goal in the first derby at Tynecastle came on the hour, from Gordon Hunter lurking as he does sometimes at the far post. The Hibs' support celebrated in the sun—the Alfresco End at Tynecastle is one of the few places where you can still do that. It was not an altogether dominant performance, but as Roddy

Gordon Hunter sweeps the ball past Andy Goram for Hibs' equaliser against Rangers

Mackenzie wrote, 'Hibs know there is no justice in derby matches, but this time they don't care'.

There was also an early win against Rangers to savour, despite the lack of refereeing breaks again. Rangers led by the only goal at the interval, and restarted with Hateley at centre-half. Hateley's first contribution of note there was to sweep the legs from Gareth Evans inside the penalty area, but the free kick was given outside. Justice was done when Hunter repeated his Tynecastle goal by sweeping O'Neill's cross behind Goram. Basille Boli, Rangers' French defender, should have been off for a dreadful double lunge at Harper, but near the end he was for tripping Evans. In between, the diminutive Kevin Harper outjumped Goram and everyone else to head Hibs' winner. After ten games, Hibs were second with Motherwell, two points behind Rangers.

Then followed a series of nine draws in ten games, the odd one out being another derby win. Darren Jackson scored two early goals, and should have made it three halfway through the first half with just the goalkeeper to beat. Hearts got a late penalty and a flattering scoreline of 2–1. After sixteen games, Hibs had just one defeat, but were trailing Rangers by eight points and Motherwell by three. However, Pat McGinlay had returned from Celtic, this time for an agreed figure of £420,000, so that the midfield was strengthened, even when Brian Hamilton crossed the city to Tynecastle after the New Year.

A Goal to Remember

A sequence of draws need not necessarily be dull, and Hibs run was spiced by some attractive football, and one goal in particular. Hibs had lost an early goal against Motherwell at Easter Road, and fought back to deserve their equaliser by McAllister on the half-hour. Shortly before the interval, McAllister brought the ball out of the Hibs' defence. Ahead of him was a row of three defenders, and the only Hibs' player, Kevin Harper, wide on the right. In a twinkling, McAllister had found Harper at speed, and he, with a single touch, flighted a cross behind the retreating defence where Michael O'Neill arrived from nowhere to hit the ball on the full volley from eighteen yards and leave Stephen Woods in goal helpless.

That was only two touches from deep inside Hibs' half, and the crowd was stunned—there was a moment's silence before the celebrations got under way. The final score was 2–2, and it took a magnificent save from a free-kick by Leighton to keep it that way.

Hibs lost at Ibrox on Boxing Day and Tynecastle in the re-arranged Ne'erday derby, but they hammered Dundee United again, this time

Kevin Harper speeds past Motherwell defenders watched by referee Waddell

A delightful cloudscape as Hibs and Falkirk players pay tribute to Kenny McLean

4–0 on Hogmanay, in a game even more one-sided than the first one. They were involved with Motherwell in a race for the remaining UEFA Cup place, the first having gone to Raith Rovers for winning the Skol Cup, and they also had an extended cup run.

The cup journey took them first to Montrose, where they had an uneasy 2–0 win, and then a dour battle at home to Motherwell for the same score. The third tie took Hibs to Ochilview, for a game whose profile had been raised by Stenhousemuir's defeats of St Johnstone and Aberdeen. Hibs turned in a professional performance that Terry Christie's team had no answer to, and won 4–0. An innovation was the provision of screens at Murrayfield Ice rink for those who could not get tickets.

The semi-final was against Celtic at Ibrox. The first game did not produce a goal, although it nearly did when McGinlay's tackle outside the penalty area resulted in a spot kick. Leighton saved Walker's kick and Hibs' skins, but he was unable to do a repeat in the replay, when Hibs were generally outplayed for Celtic to win 3–1.

Back in the league race, Hibs did themselves a big favour when they beat Motherwell 2–0, but they could not quite catch the Fir Park team, and their chances seemed to have gone when Falkirk beat them 2–0 at Easter Road. It was a sad day, because the game was started late after a minute's silence in respect for Kenny McLean who had died a few days earlier.

Hibs did not give up however; Pat McGinlay scored in the final seconds to give Hibs victory at Tannadice, and Weir, Wright and Harper scored three in seven second-half minutes for their third win against Hearts. But they had to win their last two games too, and a draw with Celtic ended their chances. Hibs finished by winning at Kilmarnock, Motherwell by losing at home to Aberdeen, so Hibs were pipped by a point from European qualification by a team they had now lost to one occasion in the last seventeen.

— 13 —
THE FOURTH EASTER ROAD

The subject of where Hibs would finally settle has rumbled on for five years or more. In Hibs' case there were two reasons why Easter Road in its existing form would not do any longer—the Taylor report, which decreed that all grounds holding more than ten thousand spectators must be all-seated by 1994 was one, and the problems following the demise what had been Edinburgh Hibernian plc was another. With Hearts intent on moving and Mercer's talking about it, the subject was seldom out of the news.

During season 1990–91, it seemed that if there was any way to extricate Hibs from the financial morass they were in, it would be at the cost of losing Easter Road, and the local authority was very constructive in working with the club to develop Meadowbank into a suitable venue for Premier League games. A move to Meadowbank seemed to be part of every proposed solution in the wrangling between Tom Farmer and his pro-Hibs faction and the Rowland camp. An expanded Meadowbank was also part of the proposal if Kenny Waugh had regained control of the club.

When Farmer finally bought Hibs and Easter Road, the options became different. The new owner made it clear that although the club no longer owned the stadium, they were welcome to stay there as long as they liked. Time was short, but by November, the fledgling board had architects studying Easter Road, which was the board's stated preference. However, that option would have meant 'a dramatic reduction in the quality and quantity of the seating at the new stadium'. A new project, at Straiton, seemed better, and in January, a £25 million scheme was announced.

Hearts' bid for permission to build at Millerhill had been turned down, and in addition a local farmer had refused to sell so that there would have been a piggery at the home end, and so Hearts were invited

Construction of the South Stand, July 1995

The construction of the new South Stand with the front rows below pitch level, July 1995

The North Stand takes shape, July 1995

to share Straiton. It did not seem likely that Mercer would agree, but it enabled him to issue more quotes. 'that is a matter for our shareholders to decide' said the owner of more than three quarters of the shares, and 'the only reason we are moving is because Edinburgh District Council wish us to move', one in the eye for those cynics who thought there might be an ulterior property motive.

By the autumn of 1992, the EDC planning director was wanting Hibs and Hearts to share at Ingliston, of which there was never much chance, and by December, it was reportedly 'virtually certain' that Hibs, with outline permission granted, would be moving to Straiton. Meanwhile, another Hearts' plan, this another one for Hermiston, was rejected. By April, and in the face of increasing disquiet among the supporters who would have to travel to Straiton, it was explained that, although only £4 million of the required £10.5 million for the scaled down version of Straiton was in place, it would be easier to finance than a £5.5 million facelift at Easter Road.

The financing and viability of the project, together with problems over the detailed planning consent, the feelings of the supporters and the timescale imposed by the football authorities finally took their toll and the board decided that after all, it would be better all round to stay at Easter Road. The announcement was made in November 1994—a first phase of two new stands at either end costing around £4.4 million to bring the capacity of the ground to about sixteen thousand. The financing came in equal measure from a bank loan and a Football Trust grant, with extras provided by Mr Farmer.

Important new facilities under the new North Stand will be a much improved retail shop, with an expanded range of merchandise and three large function suites, fitted out to exceedingly high standards. The Hibernian F.C. museum, to exhibit to supporters, school parties, tourists and others the colourful history of the club, and its place in the social history of Edinburgh and Leith was intended to be housed there too, but will instead finally be sited under the new West Stand which will replace the existing structure sooner rather than later. The museum is to be run by a committee chaired by Tom O'Malley, and including the two curators, Tom Wright and Kenny Barclay. At the time of writing, the exact timetable is undecided, and upon it will depend whether the museum starts life there or in temporary accommodation in the small building constructed at the north-west corner of the ground which will also house a television interview studio overlooking the pitch. Particular exhibitions and displays may well also take place in one of the new function suites. Although the physical location has yet to take shape, the museum is a member of the Scottish Museums Council, which will help to ensure that it is run in an efficient and professional way, and provide a lasting attraction to visitors.

The visitors' end will be less ambitious, with a police communication centre the main feature apart from the spectating facilities. There is the question of whether this too should be for home supporetrs, with the east terracing in its present form for visiting supporters—a lot depends on the how the club performs and whether it can as a result count on a home support of twelve thousand, leaving only four thousand for visitors.

Another part of the general upgrading of the stadium will be the final eradication of the famous slope. It will not be permissable in future to play European ties on sloping pitches, an edict presumably supported by Bayern München, Barcelona, Real Madrid, Napoli and the Sporting Club of Portugal among others. The intention is that the pitch will be levelled in 1996, anticipating Hibs' return to Europe that autumn. Until then Easter Road will be the only stadium with subterranean seats; since the new south stand has been constructed with the pitch levelling in mind, the front few rows are below the present level of the top end of the pitch.

We can look forward to the new flat pitch at Easter Road with the memory of the re-opening of the rugby pitch at Meggetland a few years ago when that pitch too had just been levelled. Jim Aitken, the Scottish grand slam captain, skippered the celebrity fifteen who hanselled the new-look ground, and won the toss. 'We'll play uphill first half' was his decision.

The impressive New North Stand

– Appendix 1 –
THE STATISTICS
(from 1985)

1. European Tournaments

1988-89 UEFA	1st rd.	v Videoton (HUN) (h)	1-0 ; 3-0
	2nd	v FC Liege (BEL) (h)	0-0 ; 0-1 aet
1991-92 UEFA	1st	v Anderlecht (BEL) (h)	2-2 ; 1-1 ag

2. Scottish Cup

1985-86	3rd rd.	v Dunfermline Athletic (h)	2-0
	4th	v Ayr United (h)	1-0
	5th	v Celtic (h)	4-3
	SF	v Aberdeen (n)	0-1
1986-87	3rd	v Dunfermline Athletic (h)	2-0
	4th	v Clydebank (a)	0-1
1987-88	3rd	v Dumbarton (a)	0-0, 3-0
	4th	v Celtic (a)	0-0, 0-1
1988-89	3rd	v Brechin City (h)	1-0
	4th	v Motherwell (h)	2-1
	5th	v Alloa Athletic (h)	1-0
	SF	v Celtic (n)	1-3
1989-90	3rd	v Brechin City (a)	2-0
	4th	v East Fife (h)	5-1
1990-91	3rd	v Clyde (a)	2-0
	4th	v St Johnstone (a)	1-2
1991-92	3rd	v Partick Thistle (h)	2-0
	4th	v Clydebank (a)	5-1
	5th	v Airdrie (h)	2-0
1992-93	3rd	v St Mirren (h)	5-2
	4th	v Cowdenbeath (a)	0-0, 1-0
	5th	v St Johnstone (h)	2-0
	SF	v Aberdeen (n)	0-1
1993-94	3rd	v Clyde (h)	2-1

	4th	v Hearts (h)	1-2
1994-95	3rd	v Montrose (a)	2-0
	4th	v Motherwell (h)	2-0
	5th	v Stenhousemuir (a)	4-0
	SF	v Celtic (Ibrox)	0-0, 1-3

3. Premier Results

	1985-86	1986-87	1987-88	1988-89	1989-90
Aberdeen	1-1,0-3	1-1,0-4	0-2,1-1	1-2,0-0	0-3,0-1
	0-1,0-4	1-1,0-1	0-0,2-0	1-2,0-2	3-2,2-1
Celtic	0-5,1-1	0-1,1-5	0-1,1-1	3-1,0-1	0-3,1-3
	2-2,0-2	1-4,0-1	0-2,0-2	1-3,0-1	1-0,1-1
Clydebank	5-0,4-2	3-2,0-0			
	2-3,3-1	4-1,2-1			
Dundee	2-1,0-1	0-3,0-3	0-4,1-2	1-1,1-2	3-2,0-0
	1-0,1-3	2-2,0-2	2-1,0-0	1-1,2-1	1-1,0-2
Dundee United	0-1,2-2	1-1,0-1	0-1,2-1	1-1,1-1	2-0,0-1
	1-2,0-4	0-2,1-2	0-0,2-1	1-2,1-4	0-0,0-1
Dunfermline Athletic			4-0,3-3		2-2,0-0
			2-0,0-1		2-1,1-1
Falkirk		1-0,1-1	1-0,1-1		
		2-0,3-1	0-0,0-1		
Hamilton Acads		1-3,4-1		1-0,3-0	
		1-1,1-0		2-1,3-0	
Hearts	0-0,1-2	1-3,1-1	2-1,0-1	0-0,2-1	1-1,0-1
	1-2,1-3	2-2,1-2	0-0,0-0	1-0,1-3	1-2,0-2
Morton			0-0,3-3		
			3-1,1-1		
Motherwell	1-0,0-2	0-0,1-4	1-0,0-1	1-0,1-1	3-2,2-0
	4-0,1-3	0-1,1-2	1-1,2-0	2-0,0-0	1-2,0-1
Rangers	1-3,2-1	2-1,0-3	1-0,0-1	0-1,0-0	2-0,0-3
	1-1,1-3	0-0,1-1	0-2,1-1	0-1,0-1	0-0,1-0
St Mirren	2-3,3-1	0-1,1-3	1-1,2-2	2-0,2-0	2-1,0-0
	3-0,2-0	1-0,1-1	0-0,1-1	1-0,1-3	0-1,1-0

	1990-91	1991-92	1992-93	1993-94	1994-95
Aberdeen	1-1,0-2	1-0,1-1	1-3,0-3	2-1,2-1	2-2,0-0
	2-4,0-2	1-1,1-1	1-2,0-0	3-1,3-2	4-2,0-0
Airdrie		2-2,1-0	2-2,0-2		
		0-2,3-0	3-1,1-3		
Celtic	0-3,0-2	1-1,0-1	1-2,3-2	1-1,1-1	1-1,0-2
	0-2,1-1	0-2,2-1	3-1,1-2	0-0,0-1	1-1,2-2
Dundee			0-0,1-1	2-0,2-3	
			1-3,1-3	2-1,0-4	

Dundee United	0-0,0-1	1-0,1-1	2-1,0-1	2-0,2-2	5-0,0-0
	1-0,0-0	3-2,0-1	2-1,3-0	0-1,0-3	4-0,1-0
Dunfermline Athletic	1-1,1-1	3-0,2-1			
	3-0,1-1	5-0,0-0			
Falkirk		2-2,2-3	3-1,1-2		2-2,0-0
		0-1,3-2	1-1,3-3		0-2,0-1
Hearts	0-3,1-1	1-1,0-0	0-0,0-1	0-2'0-1	2-1,1-0
	1-4,1-3	1-2,1-1	0-0,0-1	0-0,1-1	3-1,0-2
Kilmarnock				2-1,1-1	0-0,0-0
				0-0,3-0	2-1,2-1
Motherwell	1-0,1-4	0-0,1-1	2-2,2-1	3-2,2-0	2-2,1-1
	1-1,0-1	0-0,1-1	1-0,0-0	0-2,0-0	2-0,0-0
Partick Thistle			1-0,2-2	0-0,0-0	3-0,2-2
			0-1,3-0	5-1,0-1	1-2,2-2
Raith Rovers				3-2,2-1	
				3-0,1-1	
Rangers	0-0,0-4	0-3,2-4	0-0,0-1	0-1,1-2	2-1,0-2
	0-2,0-0	1-3,0-2	3-4,0-3	1-0,0-2	1-1,1-3
St Johnstone	1-0,1-1	2-1,1-0	3-1,1-1	0-0,3-1	
	0-1,0-0	0-1,1-1	2-2,0-2	0-0,2-2	
St Mirren	1-0,0-1	4-1,1-0			
	4-3,0-1	0-0,1-0			

4. Scottish League Cup

1985-86	2nd	v Cowdenbeath (h)	6-0
	3rd	v Motherwell (h)	6-1
	4th	v Celtic (h)	4-4 won on pens
	SF	v Rangers (h)	2-0, 0-1
	F	v Aberdeen (n)	0-3
1986-87	2nd	v East Stirlingshire (h)	1-0
	3rd	v Hamilton Acads. (a)	1-0
	4th	v Dundee United (h)	0-2
1987-88	2nd	v Montrose (h)	3-2
	3rd	v Queen of the South (h)	3-1
	4th	v Motherwell (a)	0-1
1988-89	2nd	v Stranraer (h)	4-0
	3rd	v Kilmarnock (h)	1-0
	4th	v Aberdeen (h)	1-2 aet
1989-90	2nd	v Alloa Athletic (h)	2-0
	3rd	v Clydebank (h)	0-0 won on pens
	4th	v Dunfermline Athletic (h)	1-3 aet

1990-91	2nd	v Meadowbank Thistle (a)	1-0
	3rd	v Raith Rovers (a)	0-1
1991-92	2nd	v Stirling Albion (a)	3-0
	3rd	v Kilmarnock (a)	3-2
	4th	v Ayr United (a)	2-0
	SF	v Rangers (Hampden)	1-0
	F	v Dunfermline Athletic (Hampden)	2-0
1992-93	2nd	v Raith Rovers (h)	4-1
	3rd	v Kilmarnock (a)	1-3
1993-94	2nd	v Alloa Athletic (h)	2-0
	3rd	v Dundee (h)	2-1
	4th	v Partick Thistle (a)	2-2 won pens
	SF	v Dundee United (n)	1-0
	F	v Rangers (n)	1-2
1994-95	2nd	v Queen of the South (a)	3-0
	3rd	v Dunfermline Athletic (h)	2-0
	4th	v Airdrieonians (h)	1-2
1995-96	2nd	v Stenhousemuir (h)	3-1
	3rd	v Airdrieonians (a)	0-2

5. League Position

1985-86	Premier League	8th
1986-87	"	9th
1987-88	"	6th
1988-89	"	5th
1989-90	"	7th
1990-91	"	9th
1991-92	"	5th
1992-93	"	7th
1993-94	"	5th
1994-95	"	3rd

6. Hat-trick Heroes

21/8/85	Steve Cowan (v Cowdenbeath, league cup)	3
28/8285	Gordon Durie (v Motherwell, league cup)	3
1/10/85	Steve Cowan (v Clydebank, league)	3
12/3/86	Steve Cowan (v St Mirren, league)	3
4/1/92	Keith Wright (v Dunfermline, league)	3
10/4/93	Keith Wright (v Dundee United, league)	3
31/12/94	Keith Wright (v Dundee United, league)	3

7. *Leading Scorers*

	League			Total	
1985-86	Steve Cowan	16		Steve Cowan	23
1986-87	George McCluskey	9		George McCluskey	9
1987-88	Paul Kane	10		Paul Kane	12
1988-89	Steve Archibald	13		Steve Archibald	16
1989-90	Keith Houchen	8		Keith Houchen	12
1990-91	Paul Wright	6		Paul Wright	6
1991-92	Mickey Weir	11		Keith Wright	17
1992-93	Darren Jackson	13		Darren Jackson	15
1993-94	Keith Wright	16		Keith Wright	19
1994-95	Keith Wright	10		Michael O'Neill	14
	Darren Jackson	10			
	Michael O'Neill	10			

8. *East of Scotland Shield*

1985-86	v Hearts (h)	1-2
1986-87	v Hearts (a)	2-0
1987-88	v Hearts (h)	1-5
1988-89	v Hearts (a)	3-3 Lost on pens
1989-90	v Hearts (h)	0-0 Won on pens
1990-91	v Hearts (a)	3-0
1991-92	v Hearts (h)	0-0 Hibs on pens
1992-93	v Hearts (a)	0-1
1993-94	v Hearts (h)	2-1
1994-95	v Hearts (a)	1-1 Lost on pens

9. *Players Honoured* (all players capped since 1985-86)

Scotland

Collins, John (4) — 1988 v SAR; 90 v EG, POL (sub), MAL

Goram, Andy (13) — 1989 v YUG, IT; 1990 v EG, POL, MAL, 1991 v ROM (2), SWZ, BUL (2), RUS, SM (2)

Jackson, Darren (7) — 1995 v RUS, SM, JAP, ECU, FI; 1996 v GR, FIN

Leighton, Jim (11) — 1994 v MAL, A, HOL; 1995 v GR, RUS, SM, JAP, ECU, FI; 1996 v GR, FIN

Macleod, Murdo (2) — 1991 v SWZ, USSR

Rough, Alan (2) — 1986 v WAL, ENG

Wright, Keith (1) — 1992 v NI

Northern Ireland

O'Neill, Michael (2) — 1994 v LCH; 1995 v EIR

Scotland "B"

Jackson, Darren	1995 v NI
McGinlay, Pat	1995 v NI
Tweed, Stephen	1995 v NI

Scotland U21

Collins, John (8)	1988 v BEL,ENG,NOR: 1989 v YUG, FR; 1990 v YUG, FR, NOR
Findlay, Billy (6)	1991 v ROM,SWZ,BUL (2), POL, USA
Hamilton, Brian (2)	1990 v FR,NOR
Harper, Kevin (2)	1996 v RUS,FIN
Hunter, Gordon (3)	1987 v EIR; 1988 v BEL, ENG (sub)
Love, Graeme (1)	1995 v RUS
May, Eddie (2)	1989 v YUG (sub), FR
Miller, Willie (7)	1991 v ROM, SWZ, BUL, POL, FR, USA; 1992 v ROM
Reid, Chris (3)	1993 v SWZ, POR, IT
Tweed, Steven (2)	1994 v SWZ, IT
Tortolano, Joe (2)	1987 v WG, EIR

— Appendix 2 —
THE TWO OF HEARTS, THE FAMOUS FIVE, THE FOUR OF HIBS

This appendix deals with a few oddities concerning Hibs through the years. The first one concerns Hearts.

1. *The Two of Hearts*

The city rivalry of Hibs and Hearts goes back to 1875 as described in the text, and of all the famous pairs of city rivals around the country, only the County and Forest of Nottingham provide an older example. After a hundred and twenty years, it is not a burning issue which of the two clubs is in fact the older; most people would take the '1874' on the Hearts crest as a clue, but they would be wrong.

There is no doubt that Hibs were formed in August 1875. The more involved argument involves Hearts, and is in two parts - firstly that the (original) Heart of Midlothian club was formed in 1875 and not 1874 as per crest, and secondly that the present Heart of Midlothian club is not the same one, but was formed under a different name, also in 1875. The evidence comes largely (see (d) below) from contemporary newspaper reports and Albert Mackie's *History of Hearts* from about 1958.

The arguments showing that the original Heart of Midlothian club was formed in 1875 are several, as follows :-

(a) The break-up of the former club White Star, whose members founded both Hibs and Hearts, took place in 1875, as recounted in John Rafferty's *One Hundred Years of Scottish Football*.
(b) *Scottish Sport* printed a history of Edinburgh football, only a few years after the event, and was sufficiently sure of its ground to give Hearts' first match as 28th August 1875, against 3rd ERV, and

listed teams, score and scorers. *The Scotsman* confirms that that match took place on that date.

(c) All the early SFA records give 1875 as the formation of the original Hearts. Given the readiness of early Hearts' secretaries of the time to point out perceived errors in scores etc. to the newspapers, it is unlikely that the date was an error and was not highlighted as such.

(d) The recollections of John Cochrane as told by Mackie. Cochrane was 83 years of age when his memory was tapped, but newspaper reports back up his stories, except that he was consistently about two years out. In particular, he recalled being with a club called St. Andrews in 1874 when Hearts, who had been in existence for about a year, disbanded. This is used by Mackie to corroborate Tom Purdie's claim that Hearts were formed in 1873. In fact, it was in September 1876 that *The Scotsman* noted that Hearts had broken up 'owing to deficiency of membership' thus corroborating the date as 1875.

(e) there is no mention in newspapers of Heart of Midlothian before August 1875, although other sides of little consequence were reported from time to time.

The second part of the argument goes as follows. According to Cochrane, he was attending a regular meeting of the St Andrew's club in an Edinburgh hotel shortly after the Hearts break-up when three Hearts players arrived, asked to join the club, and were accepted as playing members. They were Purdie, Mitchell and Lees. Cochrane then claims that a vote was taken to change the name of the club to Heart of Midlothian, and this was done.

Again, *The Scotsman* backs this up, except for the timing. Certainly as early as October 14th, the St Andrews team which faced Swifts included the three ex-Hearts men, but they continued to play under the name of St Andrew's for some months - it is not until January 1877 that the name of Heart of Midlothian reappears in place of St Andrew's. Cochrane further recalled going with Hearts to play a cup-tie against a Dundee team in Kirkcaldy and having to take the goal posts with them, which clearly relates to the 'Edinburgh St Andrews versus Dundee St. Clements' tie which took place at Kirkcaldy on the 21st October 1876.

Clearly then, the roots of the present Hearts lie with the St Andrews club and not the original Heart of Midlothian club. It is clear from Cochrane's account that it was not a merger. This is supported implicitly by *The Scotsman* inasmuch as before their disbanding, Hearts were one of the club featured in reviews of the season etc. whereas at the end of season 1876-77, the former St Andrews/new Hearts club was not mentioned. (even if it had been a merger, the new club would surely have had a starting date of 1876).

The formation of St Andrews is not well documented. However, we do know that the early S.F.A records give their date of formation also as 1875.

Secondly, as they did not join the S.F.A. and were not included in the Edinburgh Cup draw made on September 25th 1875, at which Dunfermline were admitted to membership and the Edinburgh Cup competition, they were probably not in existence at that time.

Thirdly, although many matches between exceedingly minor teams were reported in *The Scotsman*, no mention is made of St. Andrews until well into 1876, which suggests they were formed very late in 1875.

There are therefore two conclusions; Hearts were certainly formed in 1875, not 1874 as their crest shows, and the balance of probabilities indicates that Hibs are the older club, contrary to conventional wisdom.

2. *The Famous Five*

The Famous Five of Smith, Johnstone, Reilly, Turnbull and Ormond trips off the tongue of all Hibs supporters old enough to have seen them. The first time that that quintet played together was against Nithsdale Wanderers in a friendly match in Sanquhar in 1948. However, the first time that the Hibs forward line read Smith, Johnstone, Reilly, Turnbull, Ormond was during the 1947 tour of Scandinavia - when the Johnstone in question was Leslie, who was signed at great expense from Clyde and was sold back to them within a year.

Another coincidence of names is that in 1960-61, Hibs success against the likes of Barcelona was in no small measure due to Joe Baker and Johnny Macleod, both of whom were transferred away in 1961. The players brought in to replace them had by chance the same names, Gerry Baker and Ally McLeod. Gerry was of course Joe's brother, and father of the athlete Lorraine Baker, and Ally made a name for himself in Argentina.

3. The Four of Hibs

The number of occasions in senior Scottish, or for that matter, British football on which father and son have played for the same club is quite small, but during the 1980s, a curious situation occurred at Easter Road which is almost certainly unique.

In the middle part of the eighties, Hibs had both Joe McBride, the winger whose father Joe snr. had come from Celtic in the late sixties, and Paul Kane, son of Jimmy Kane, whose career as an inside forward in the late fifties had come to an abrupt end in a clash with the Aberdeen goalkeeper Tubby Ogston.

Then in 1987, Hibs signed Andy Goram, whose father Lew had been an understudy to Jimmy Kerr around 1950, and whose performance in a match at Easter Road while on loan to Third Lanark was a factor in Hibs not winning the league championship that year. When Andy arrived, Hibs therefore fielded three players in the same XI whose fathers had played for the club.

Next, Joe McBride Jr moved on, but Mark McGraw came from Morton, where his father, a striker with Morton and Hibs in the sixties, was manager. Goram, Kane and McGraw all played in the same Hibs' XI

Moreover, all three were still there when Murdo Macleod came from Borussia Dortmund as player/assistant manager. Now Murdo's father played for Hibs around the outbreak of the Second World War. With the others, therefore Hibs then fielded teams including no fewer than four players whose fathers had played for the club - surely a record.